THE STARLING'S SURPRISE

How MEADOWBROOK HIGH SCHOOL, ST. ANDREW JAMAICA
Won 7 Trophies in 4 years in the 1980's
by
Glaister Lancelot Prince
MEADOWBROOK MEMORIES ©®TM

The Starling's Surprise: How Meadowbrook High School, St. Andrew Jamaica Won 7 Trophies In 4 Years In The 1980's

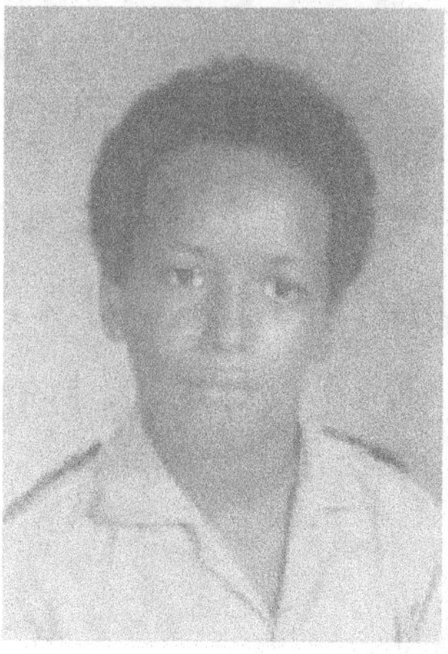

Glaister Lancelot Prince, Author

Front Cover Pictures
Top: Starlings
Bottom: Meadowbrook High School Sunlight Cup Winner Cricket Team 1982
Standing (Left to Right)

Graham Rhoden, Lloyd "Piggy" Williams (vice-captain), Dane Miller, Christopher Cheddar, Timon Waugh, Michael "TC" Hall, Glaister "Jelly" Prince (Captain), Hopeton "Hitchy" Burke, Standford "Goosey" Brown, Mike"The Dread" Hare (coach)
Stooping from left to right
Gary Simms, Noel Curtis, Leon Johnson, Kevin Reese, Bryon Nunes, Devon McDonald, Hugh Green, Garfield Marston, Clive Edwards.

Meadowbrook High School Tartan

Motto " Let Your Light So Shine"

SUNLIGHT CUP PRESENTATION TO OUR PRINCIPAL Ms. C. L McCLENNON

A proud Principal Ms McClennon being presented the Sunlight Cup by skipper Glaister (Jelly) Prince surrounded by members of the history making 1982 Sunlight Cup Team .

MEADOWBROOK MEMORIES

Memories of Former Principal Ms. C.L McLennon

YOUTUBE LINKS BELOW FOR SCAN QR CODES
FROM TOP LEFT

1. Meadowbrook memories YouTube channel

https://youtube.com/@meadowbrookmemories9244?si=JoHzCr4Ip_C5N5En

2. MM # 1 Maurice Minott

https://youtu.be/40zNf331WGE?si=88ZeR6JUbKWrSuqw

3. MM # 13 Colin Channer

https://youtu.be/cr2-NVJJhxo?si=PI7Z0cntOIWNWvFm

4. MM #15 Glaister Prince

https://youtu.be/wwOnFyZxau8?si=tBW_uH4Tdir2Z43H

5. MM # 32 Mikhail Hamilton

https://youtu.be/mVHpL_BA-Ak?si=3y33jM65dxueRFxy

6. MM # 42 Donald Bogle

https://youtu.be/WoJ6x8TS_Iw?si=7UO4lDmr4voCTc3K

7. MM # 55 Maureen Yearwood (Spence)

https://youtu.be/j0DgN3ewF8c?si=VbYMMOumWzILG9sv

8. MM # 59 The Wright Sisters (Karen , Andrea and Beverley)

https://youtu.be/B7jPyyUJU4A?si=Bod0dhU3z7nwKK8N

9. MM # 71 Martin Brown

https://youtu.be/Hh1xOGZyLoM?si=0m6qH8BfgPTxult4

10. MM # 74 Sefton (Gully) Letts, Rohan (Salla)Lewis, Sean (Ryder) Terrell, Trevor (Tego)Lamb and Stephen (Cluck) Coombs

https://youtu.be/5i67z-W8u2Q?si=cMbUDCN_tfZvgGbH

11. MM # 78 Kevin Facey (Current Principal)

https://youtu.be/lrXkUDF7IcY?si=gmoKS1B3IMFWxFp1

12. MM # 100 Memories of C L McClennon

https://youtu.be/UW-6ZNEUgQI?si=h1431PF51GRgKSHy

TABLE OF CONTENTS

ACKNOWLEDGEMENTS

First, I would like to thank the founders and visionaries who started that small school, MEADOWBROOK HIGH SCHOOL St. Andrew Jamaica, in 1958. Reverend Henry Ward and Reverend Madge Saunders are two of the many names that were pivotal in the birth of our School. It was the nurturing and free-spirited environment of our school that inspired us to reach heights BEYOND ANY BOUNDARY which is embedded in our school Motto (Ita Splendeat Lvx Vestra) "Let Your Light So Shine".

This means that everyone associated with MEADOWBROOK is allowed to shine in their own individual way, and when we serendipitously team up the results are ever so magical.

Special thanks to the entire Meadowbrook High School Community (past, current and future) whose love and support for all things MEADOWBROOK makes the journey of writing this book very joyful.

It's impossible to list individually everyone whom I wish to thank but the few specific persons I wish to thank, are as follows: Carlton Facey and Donovan Thomas (Tegre or Don T) who reached out to me when I was visiting Jamaica in 2016 which was my inspiration to go down the road of Meadowbrook Memories.

Also, my good friends Wayne Fuller, Douglas Crooks and Christopher Cheddar gave me support whenever I needed it. Anthony Moore, notably, never stopped believing in my dreams and always provided tremendous encouragement.

My newfound friend, Margaret Livermore was a reminder of the power of female participation in our Meadowbrook community. My mentor and friend for over 42 years was a senior manager for ESSO STANDARD OIL, the company that feted and honored Meadowbrook's first winning Sunlight Cup Team.

It is his discourses which made me question my biases and push me to formulate ideas and theories as they continue to evolve in my quest to be just a little bit better every day.

The first coach and mentor who made me realize that merit -based selection will outperform any other selection criteria was Mr. Neville Beckford (Becky). The coach who inspired me to believe in myself by entrusting me with an unexpected leadership role, and whose endorsement of my cricketing ability years later (in an email exchange in 2016) made me feel like I had received a Knighthood, was Mr. Michael Hare (The Dread).

To Dr. Lindsay O'Brien Quarrie, a Meadowbrook Alum, who took the time to provide the final editing and publishing challenge to get this book past the finish line, I extend my sincere thanks.

FOREWORD

Glaister aka Jelly aka Lance Prince and I crossed paths at Meadowbrook High School in the 1980s. He was a little older than me and we had no interaction then. Fast forward to April 2022 when I clicked on a link titled Meadowbrook Memories and what I heard was so intriguing and hilarious I was hooked. I started listening and realized the female perspective of the Meadowbrook Memories was missing and reached out to him. He challenged me to get females to share their memories (as many refused), I took up the challenge and the rest is history. Please check out the Meadowbrook Memories podcast on Youtube. You can thank me later. 😁
https://youtube.com/@meadowbrookmemories9244?si=JoHzCr4Ip_C5N5En

When Prince shared THE STARLING'S SURPRISE - How MEADOWBROOK High School won 7 Trophies in 4 years in the 1980s in Jamaica, I wasn't sure what to expect. What I discovered was a real treasure. It can be viewed as a playbook for creating success in all aspects of your life. Prince leaves no stones unturned as he shares stories about Mr. Hare "The Dread" and his cohorts (other teachers and parents) building the cricket team from scratch in 1978 resulting in a team that shocked Jamaica and the schoolboy cricket community by winning multiple trophies in the 1980s.

His use of language transports us to the school's campus and we feel the strenuous workouts, motivational speeches and the heartbreak when harsh discipline was meted out. The excitement, energy, camaraderie and family atmosphere of that time is palpable; the reader feels like they can touch, smell and feel it.

Starlings are small birds that are often overlooked. However they are strong, intelligent creatures that learn quickly and work well as a team. They are also known for their ability to outcompete native birds for food and limited resources.

This book is a must have for all Meadowbrookians and I hope it becomes a must read for students and teachers at Meadowbrook for years to come, as it contains many valuable lessons that will never become obsolete and documents by example

the outcome of dedication, commitment and the rise like starlings to achieve personal and collective goals and success.

Maragaret Livermore, December 2023, Meadowbrook High School Class of 1983

DEDICATION

This book is dedicated to my grandson ZHYLO PRINCE and my granddaughter ADDILYN PRINCE who inspired me to embrace the power of forgiveness by being granted the privilege of spending a lot of time with them.

If they happen to read this book and are inspired by some of the stories they read here, I will be eternally grateful.

Glaister Lancelot Prince
February 11, 2024

PROLOGUE

The significance of what MEADOWBROOK achieved in this story was almost overlooked by me during the writing of this book . In 1982 when we created history MEADOWBROOK was still a young school. Founded in 1958 by the Reverend Henry Ward, it was only 24 years old (a young adult) compared to schools we dominated who were all founded in the first half of the 20th century and some before. We were a young upstart school who didn't have the history or tradition those older schools had, so for us to dominate and create a sporting dynasty before our school reached 30 years old was and still is a monumental achievement.

The other significant memory of our sporting achievements, particularly the internationally beloved game Cricket, is that our dominance was against the backdrop of the rise and dominance of the great West Indies Cricket team which dominated World Cricket from that famous (groveling) tour to England in 1976 to well into the 1990s . The fact that this West Indies Cricket Team was the most successful Black Sporting Team in the History of Team sports, inspired many Jamaican schoolboys to aspire to be a part of that great West Indies Team. During this time Meadowbrook cricketers were the "creme de la creme ' of school boy cricketers in Jamaica and the West Indies. The fact that none of our cricketers went on to play for the West Indies was not a lack of talent but a lack of opportunity because of the parochial selection policy by Jamaican youth cricket selectors and because MEADOWBROOK was never seen as a "brand name school ".

This point was driven home by the performance of one of Meadowbrook's great athletes Donat "Stali/Stallion" Mair . When I went to MEADOWBROOK, STALI was in fourth form and he played Sunlight Cup, Manning Cup and was a supreme Middle Distance runner (400, 800 and 1500 meters). Since track and field made it difficult for selectors to ignore your personal performance, Stali went on to represent Jamaica at the Junior Carifta games and won a GOLD medal in the 1978 Junior Carifta Games held in the Bahamas.

Stali's determination and stamina was an inspiration to tons of students who were privileged to have played and competed with him with his "never say die' attitude. Even after he graduated from Meadowbrook, he was always at 'bottom field' helping and participating in training members of those successful Evelyn Cup and Minor Cup Teams.

More than any other athlete, Stali's track and field success epitomizes the greatness of our athletes who may have gone on to achieve more if they were not slighted by questionable selection processes.

This point was reinforced when a Meadowbrook alum , Anthony "Tony" Moore (Class of 1984) recently reminded me of a match in which Carlton Facey was slapping Kingston College (KC)'s fast bowler Derion Dixon with contemptuous disdain all over the field to carry Meadowbrook to a comfortable victory. Dixon went on to represent Jamaica at the Senior level and Facey would probably have done the same if he attended a "brand name" school, such as KC.

INTRODUCTION

Meadowbrook- The Golden Years

This book was written for 3 main reasons
1) To document my personal journey as a part of the Meadowbrook team that broke the glass ceiling and started a dynasty of success that created 3 Sunlight Cup Championships, 1 Walker Cup Championship , 2 Tappin Cup Championships and a Nutrament Shield Championship within a 4 year period from 1982- 1986.
2) To pay respect to 3 unrecognized and underappreciated gentlemen who were mostly responsible for putting the infrastructure and systems in place for those Golden Years - Michael (the dread) Hare, Neville (Becky) Beckford and Rory McGregor. Without the opportunity and foundational support of these 3 men this journey would not have been possible.
3) To explain the systems that these gentlemen put in place (consciously or unconsciously) because if one knows the system, it is possible to duplicate the success experienced almost four decades ago.

Mr. Hare , Mr. Beckford and Mr. McGregor had systems in place that:
1) Always recruited new players
2) Had a training regimen that got more out of current players
3) Implemented systems that encouraged and nurtured flexibility in his cricketers (Kirkton Ebanks was recruited as a left arm spin bowler and when we won the Sunlight Cup in 1986, he was the most destructive top order batsman for that team).

These are the same systems I used, to launch and run several successful businesses over the last 35 years:
1) Always getting new customers
2) Getting existing customers to buy more frequently
3) Getting new and existing customers to buy higher value products.

The Meadowbrook experience and these true leaders continue to inspire success!.

CHAPTER 1

SUCCESS AT MEADOWBROOK HIGH SCHOOL
THE GOLDEN YEARS   1976 – 1986

In September 2016 while in Jamaica after attending my mother's funeral (she had unexpectedly died on August 19, 2016) I received a call from Carlton Facey. I had not spoken to him in over 30 years and he said he along with other past students wanted to give me a trophy for being part of the Sunlight Cup team that won the corporate area schoolboy cricket title in 1982.

I felt honored because apart from the function that ESSO STANDARD OIL had put on for us in 1982, it was almost as if this milestone in our school history was forgotten. No other recognition was ever given to that historic team of 1982. Most former players with whom I spoke still have those small replica trophies that ESSO gave us and they all seem to treasure it because it appears to be the only tangible memory we have that acknowledges that the 1982 MEADOWBROOK Sunlight Cup team were ' HISTORY MAKERS' to quote the vice-captain of that team LLOYD "piggy' WILLIAMS during a celebration following the defeat of our arch rival, CALABAR, by 64 runs.

Upon receiving my award from Donovan 'DON T or TEG REG' Thomas at Melbourne cricket club (he was the person instrumental in organizing this function to honor that team and when the original function was held I was not in Jamaica) I started thinking about how did MEADOWBROOK, a very small coeducational school, nestled under the hills on Meadowbrook Ave able to achieve the success it did in those years 1982-1986 and how come this feat has never been duplicated in the over 30 years since we last won a team competition ? We defeated KINGSTON COLLEGE (KC) in the 1986 SUNLIGHT CUP final).

During those years we won the SUNLIGHT CUP 3 times, the TAPPIN CUP twice, the WALKER CUP once and reached the semifinals in SUNLIGHT TAPPIN CUP numerous times and we also won the Walker Cup and Nutrament Shield.

A GREAT FAMILY TRADITION

Meadowbrook's success during those years is worth examining because since those years our school had not been able to duplicate the achievements that we accomplished.

My time at Meadowbrook 1974- 1982 has both historical legacy and tradition. I always wanted to attend Meadowbrook, that small school nestled under Mannings Hill and Queens Hill on Meadowbrook Ave, surrounded by willow trees which whistled on my first day in September 1974. One of my two sisters Claudette "Bibi Prince" started her school career at Meadowbrook in 1966 and graduated in 1972. My older sister Noeleen "Daun "Prince (nee Laing) attended Merle Grove.

My brother Patrick started at Meadowbrook in September 1972 (Bibi's last year) and left in 1980. I started Meadowbrook in September 1974 and left in 1982. My cousin Lorna Martin started Meadowbrook after my mother took her to Mr. Thorpe who knew our history (my sister and brother and I all attended or were attending Meadowbrook).

My cousin Richard Lodge started attending Meadowbrook in 1979 and left in 1985. His sister Sophe Lodge started attending Meadowbrook in 1982 and left in 1987.
My niece Nadia Laing (Daun's daughter started attending Meadowbrook in 1988. Her brother Dane Laing started attending Meadowbrook in 1990. Therefore, from 1966 until 1992 a member of our family has attended Meadowbrook interrupted by the school year 1987-1988.

This great tradition of our family about attending school was repeated I was living in Orlando when the Princes attended Olympia High School. From 2002 until 2017 attended Olympia uninterrupted, beginning with Sean-Patrick in 2001 and continued with Danielle (Patrick's two children) followed by Kyle, Thomas (my two sons) and finally with Arantxa (my daughter) who graduated in May 2017.

MEADOWBROOK FAMILIES I REMEMBER

Munroe (Vaughn (moochie), Lawrence (Lolis)and Shawn)

Mattis (Kirkland, Lawrence and Oswald)

Thame (Minerva and Jennifer)

Johnson (Jago(original), Lenworth and Dale)

Belvanis (Gerald and Donovan)

Goulbourne (Hugh and Howard)

Witter (Grace and Luke)

Thomas (Vivian and the late Howard)

Subadan Sisters (Claudette and Sharon)

Lewis (Heather and Marcia and Gary(lu lu)

Douet (Robert and Patrick)

Curtis (Delve, Patrick, Lyndon) , Noel (Alfanso) and Mark.

Smith (Gobblers) Patrick and Paul.

Swaby (Mark and Garth)

Jones (Cheryl,Jerry and Margaret)

Anderson (Heather and Sophie)

Keane (David , Diane and Gillian)

Ramsey (Allison, Camille and Saffron)

Strudwick (Sheena , Courtney and Janet)

Scott (Vivienne and Janette)

Harris (Hugh, Karl and Gary)

Cameron (Harold - deceased) Pat and Peter.

Jacobs (Dean and Peter)

Earle (Charmaine and Andrew)

Nunez (Enrico and Christopher)

Lindo (Andrea and Carol)

Hucey (Judith , Joan and Valerie)

Nicholson (Douglas , Nelly, Joan and Carol)

Marks (Denise and younger sister)

Chung (Richard and Ian)

Holmes (Courtney and Raymond)

Lindo (Gary and Bruce)

Beecher (Karen and Maureen)

Howell (Shawn and Michelle)

Delfosse (Melody Leighton and younger brother Patrick)

Seixas (Alan and Anthony)

Scott (Patrick and Robert)

Christian (Carlton and older sister)

Manning (Hector and Junior)

Eytle (James , Christopher, Jacqueline)

Ralf (George and Michael) brother of Sheryl Lee Ralph

Bent (Ferdinand and George)

Dewar (Dirk and Tracy)

Stewart (Michelle, Dave , younger brother)

Dietrich (Karen,Cheryl and Lisa)

Carr (Donovan and Michael)

Milwood (Karen , Eleanor and Denise)

Ebanks (Kirton and Dillion)

Bridigette Cossie and Sharon Demercado

Johnson (Jacqueline, Howard and Delroy)

White (Keith , Constance and Allison)

Banks (B and I and Hermine)

Sailsmans (Paul and Gary)

Alexander (Neville and Christopher)

Chin (Hillary and Angella)

Walker (Carol and Inger)

Garvey (Jackie and Michelle)

Chin (Gary and Karl)

Dewar (Roy and Wayne)

Forth (Judith and Peta-Gaye)

Gouldbourne (Howard and Hugh)

Mccourtie (Milton and Roy)

Delapena (Marc , Stephen and Garth)

Sexiaus (Allan and Anthony)

Scott (Patrick and michael)

Christian (Carlton and Sandra)
Wright (Karen and Andrea and Beverley)
Creary (Lesmond and Garfield)
Richards (Joy and Faith)
Mcgregror (Audley(Gilla) and Karen)

Manning (Hector and Junior)
Ralph (George and Michael)
Wildman (Hazel and Donette)
Davis (Eleanor and Michelle)
Smelie (Pauline and sister)
Sanguinetti (Christopher and Michelle)
Smith (Andre, Allison and Derek)
Phillips (Gregory , Richard and Francine)
Blair (John and Sarah)
Jacobs (Dean and Peter)
Chung (Jacqueline and Julie)
Johnson (Derek and Brian)
Cameron (Harold, Patrice and Peter)

CHAPTER 2

Cricket Lovely Cricket

I fell in love with cricket when I stumbled upon a book by Lawrence Donovan L.D (Strebor) Roberts - Cricket's Brightest Summer in the early 1970s before I started attending Meadowbrook .

This book was about the West Indian cricket team tour of Australia in 1960-1961. That team was captained by Sir Frank Worrell and included the legendary Sir Gary Sobers, Wes Hall, Lester King (whose sons LESTER TONY KING and SEAN KING attended Meadowbrook during that Golden Era 1976-1986). His grandsons also attended MEADOWBROOK HIGH (ADRIAN KING 2003-2008 and ALDEN KING 2005-2011).

The impact this book had on me was significant because it was the first time that a black man Sir Frank Worrell was captaining the West Indies Cricket team for an entire overseas tour. Previously the great George Headly may have captained the team for one or two matches in the Caribbean, but it was thought that a black man could not be trusted for the leadership position of the West Indies team for an entire series much less an overseas tour of Australia. This tour dispelled all doubts about the leadership abilities of Sir Frank Worrell as he led the team with such grace and poise that when the team departed Australia over 200,000 Australians lined the streets of Melbourne to show their support for the team.

The tour which included the first tied test match was won by Australia 2-1, but for questionable umpiring decisions from the partial Australian umpire the result of the series could have been different. After that series, Australia and the West Indies competed for the Sir Frank Worrell trophy. Although he was born in Barbados, he played for Jamaica after moving to live there in his early 20's. He was appointed a senator by Prime Minister Sir Alexander Bustamante in the 1960, and he retired in 1964 after captaining the team to its first series victory in England in 1963. He died in 1967 from leukemia at the University of the West Indies.
Sir Frank Worrell became captain mainly through the efforts of CLR James who used his influence as a writer at the Nation newspaper in Trinidad to inform and incite the Caribbean public that the racist policy of preventing a black man from

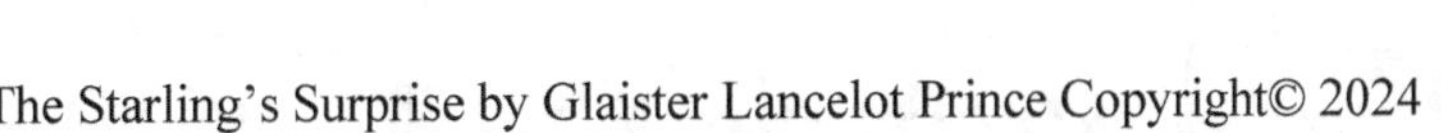

captaining the team must end, not because he was black but because he was the best man for the job.

The significance of this was not lost on me when the support and admiration that Worrell and his team got vindicated CLR James' campaign to get a black man in a significant leadership role in the Caribbean, solely on merit. This stuck and inspired me throughout my entire life as I saw cricket as a sport that if you became good enough you could rise to the top based on your own ability.

After being inspired I started listening and playing cricket on a regular basis. I remembered Lawrence Rowe's double century and his century in his first test match against New Zealand at Sabina park in 1972. I listened to every ball of the triple century he made against England in Barbados in 1974 and by the time the West Indies team toured Australia in 1975-1976, I was an avid cricket fan.

The Australian team led by Dennis Lillie and Jeff Thompson humiliated the Caribbean team by 5-1, but it was the beginning of the era of the dominance of West Indies cricket which reigned supreme in the cricketing world for the next 20 years. Roy Fredericks' 169 at Perth on that 1975-1976 tour of Australia, is still the most fascinating innings that I ever listened to (at that time there was no live TV broadcast of cricket in the Caribbean) .

The great West Indies team of that era which won the initial 2 cricket world cups in 1975 and 1979, produced a plethora of great West Indians players which further inspired me to get better and CLR James must have been proud of the dominance of a Caribbean team made up of mainly black men inspiring a generation of young Caribbean cricketers.

I also read any book I could get on the subject including CLR JAMES , seminal book BEYOND THE BOUNDARY . I subscribed to Tony Becca's monthly cricket magazine and read the story of Sir Frank Worrell's life (he died in 1967 at the age of 42). I also began playing cricket literally every day on the street without proper equipment (all we needed was a bat and a ball) .

I learned to play straight as playing on the street on Colbeck Ave in Pembroke Hall where I grew up meant two things. First the only way you could score a four was hitting the ball straight back passed the bowler and playing other shots (a hook, a square cut meant breaking the neighbors' windows and big trouble.). We also made our own bat out of any piece of wood we could find as initially we could not afford to purchase a proper cricketing bat. The ball was mainly a cork and tork ball which seemed to have been made out of steel because if you got hit with that ball anywhere on your body the pain was unbearable.

My love for cricket and Meadowbrook meant that I followed the exploits of the Meadowbrook team by reading the newspaper about the results of matches played on the weekend. I remembered one particular match where St Jago made 317 for 3 declared and bowled out Meadowbrook for a paltry 17, but that was before I was a student at Meadowbrook. The scores in that match did not resonate with me until years later when I realized that making 300 in a cricket match in one day was no mean achievement for a schoolboy cricketer and the yawning gap between Meadowbrook and other teams was embarrassingly huge.

When I started Meadowbrook in 1974 Courtney (TIDO) Holmes was captain of the Sunlight cup team and his younger brother Raymond Holmes also played on that team and also played on the colts team captained by Herbert McDonald , which also included Wilfred Rattigan. However it was the inclusion of two of my friends from when I was in first form on that team which gave me further inspiration to work harder and improve my game. (Glen CRACKING Atkins and Douglas Crooks)

CHAPTER 3

Support from Beyond the Boundary our secret weapon

1974 MY FIRST YEAR AT MEADOWBROOK HIGH SCHOOL

GLAISTER LANCELOT PRINCE

THE UNION

I started attending Meadowbrook in September 1974 after being the only one of 2 boys who passed Common Entrance from Pembroke Hall Primary. The other boy was Robert Douet who became my lifelong friend until his unfortunate death from a cross fire in a gun robbery in Jamaica sometime after I migrated in 2000. At Meadowbrook we teamed up with another lifelong friend (who had a longer name than I did) Lenworth Raymond St. Aubyn Johnson (JAGO) to create a potent disarming weapon that was successfully used throughout our glory years to inspire our team and demoralize our opponents.

Jago, Robert(Do) and I (Jelly) used our verbal acumen to disarm and at times disorient our friends and adversaries and by the time we achieved the pinnacle of team success by winning the Sunlight Cup in 1982 for the first time, our wit and voices were reinforced by past students like my brother Patrick Prince, Gerald G Belnavis and brother Donovan (member of the popular music band "Blood Fire Posse") Belvanis, Mr. Meadowbrook himself Garth Swaby, a batch mate of Donovan, teacher Rory McGregor and other cricketers like Christopher Cheddar and his father the late Sam Cheddar.

This was not an exclusive club and the only barrier to entry was that you had wit, a sense of humor and a loud voice. This group became known as the " union " and we were as hard on each other as we were on our adversaries or arch opponents. This strategy worked pretty well in cricket which was a game played over 6 hours and gave us " the union " ample time to get to upset the opposing team batsmen, bowlers or fielders. All it took was one union member to find the smallest flaw in our opponents (his hairstyle, his shoe, a midfield hiccup), anything. We would point out this flaw over and over which most times made our opponents focus on the wrong thing instead of the task at hand - the cricket match they were playing.

Three classic examples of this are illustrated in:

1) Once we were playing an Evelyn Cup match against Domtar and the opening batsman was a rotund overweight batsman. Jago began shouting out that we should

check his stomach for a missing boy who was alleged to have been eaten by a crocodile in Old Harbor earlier in the week. Needless to say that batsman did not last long.

2) Once playing a Minor Cup match against Duhaney Park . Neville "Becky" Beckford was bowling to Pat, the opening batsman from Duhaney Park. One memorable delivery was square cut so hard and with such venom by Pat that Rory who was at point had to duck for cover and did not have to retrieve the ball from the boundary because it had rebounded off the hill on the boundary. It was maybe what CLR James described in his book "Beyond the Boundary " the unkindest cut. Christopher Cheddar asked Becky about that square cut when we spoke on the phone in the early part of 2017 after not communicating with Becky for over 30 years. Yes we still remain as hard on each other as our opponent.

3) Once in a Manning Cup match against Camperdown , Thomas McLean took a free kick with Alfred "Hitchcock " Henry in goal. Hitchcock appeared to have the ball covered until as " Do" and "Jago" reminded " Hitchcock " and the rest of the union at whatever chance they got that "Hitchcock " apparently had a large hole in his heart because somehow the ball went straight through him to give Camperdown a goal which completely demoralized our team.

Any and every opportunity to sharpen our wit gave us great fun when we were players like Jago and I were, and we became a powerful weapon that was unleashed on our cricketing opponents in Sunlight, Tappin, Evelyn or Minor Cup matches on Saturdays and Sundays between 1976 and 1986.

We won many matches during those years because of the support and strength that the "Union " provided from " Beyond the Boundary ".

CHAPTER 4

Inspiration from Meadowbrook Cricketers.

In 1974 when I started Meadowbrook, Cricket and Football were our (my brother and I) favorite sports. Unfortunately that year my brother started the school year with a severe handicap, because of a serious bone disease he endured during that summer, osteomyelitis. He spent most of the summer in the university hospital and when school reopened in September he had to use a cane to walk. This did not stop him from playing football for our school house Rothnie and even with his inability to use one foot, he was easily the best player for our team. His determination to play in spite of hobbling on the football field was a memory I will not forget.

When the cricket season started in January we both played on the house team in inter house junior cricket competition and he also played for the Colts cricket team. He bowled a wicked off break and a wily leg break, but because of the operation on his foot the summer before, I think he was terrified of those tough cricket balls touching his leg, so he always appeared to be heading toward the square leg umpire. It was during the cricket season I saw 2 of the most gifted Cricketers to have ever played for Meadowbrook during my years there, Glen " cracking " Atkins and Douglas " Dougie Crooks.

Cracking and Dougie both played Sunlight and Colts cricket for Meadowbrook when they were in first form. Cracking was the best and most fearsome fast bowler I have ever seen to never play for the West Indies. Until I saw Cracking bowl, I had never seen a fast bowler with such an intimidating pace and a vicious bouncer. I never witnessed such venom playing on Colbeck Ave. He was also a very competent batsman when he concentrated and was a ferocious striker of the ball. He was the only one who seemed to have more cricket books to read than I did.

Dougie was an attacking batsman who could destroy any bowling attack with his wide range of shots. He hooked and cut the fastest of bowlers including

Cracking with consummate ease and was equally comfortable against spin bowlers. Until I saw Brian Lara play for the West Indies, I had never seen a left handed batsman who possessed such exquisite timing and range of strokes like Dougie.

Up until I played my last competitive cricket match in 1986 or 1987 I never had the confidence to play the hook shot the way Dougie did.

One year in a practice match against the Jamaican National women's Cricket team, the captain of the team and also the captain of the West Indies women cricket team Vivalyn Latty Scott made the mistake of disrespecting Cracking by telling him he was a schoolboy and he was no match to her. Cracking promptly bowled a vicious bouncer which surprised her and in her effort to get out of the way she ended up on her haunches. She immediately became docile and the battle of the sexes was settled by Cracking letting her and the rest of the schoolboys realize he could bowl a bouncer like the fastest West Indies bowlers in their prime.

Dougie's timing and abilities to dispatch the ball to any part of the ground was demonstrated in one memorable match against STATHS at Bumper Hall on Spanish town road. In one memorable stroke against the STATHS fast bowler, he chipped into the bowler and caressed the ball with such timing over his head that it sailed for a six and had to be retrieved from Spanish Town Road.

Unfortunately Dougie's eyesight started deteriorating, unknown to me until years later when he was unable to pick up the sight of the hall as quickly as he used to and he lost confidence and he chose to play less cricket in his last couple of years of high school. This was a great loss because I think if he had played on the 1981 Sunlight Cup team (my first year as captain, his final year in high school) we could have reached the semifinals so we missed getting into the semifinals then, by only one point.

Anyway the standard was set by my two friends who were playing Sunlight from first form and I only became a regular member of the team in 1980 (6 years later).

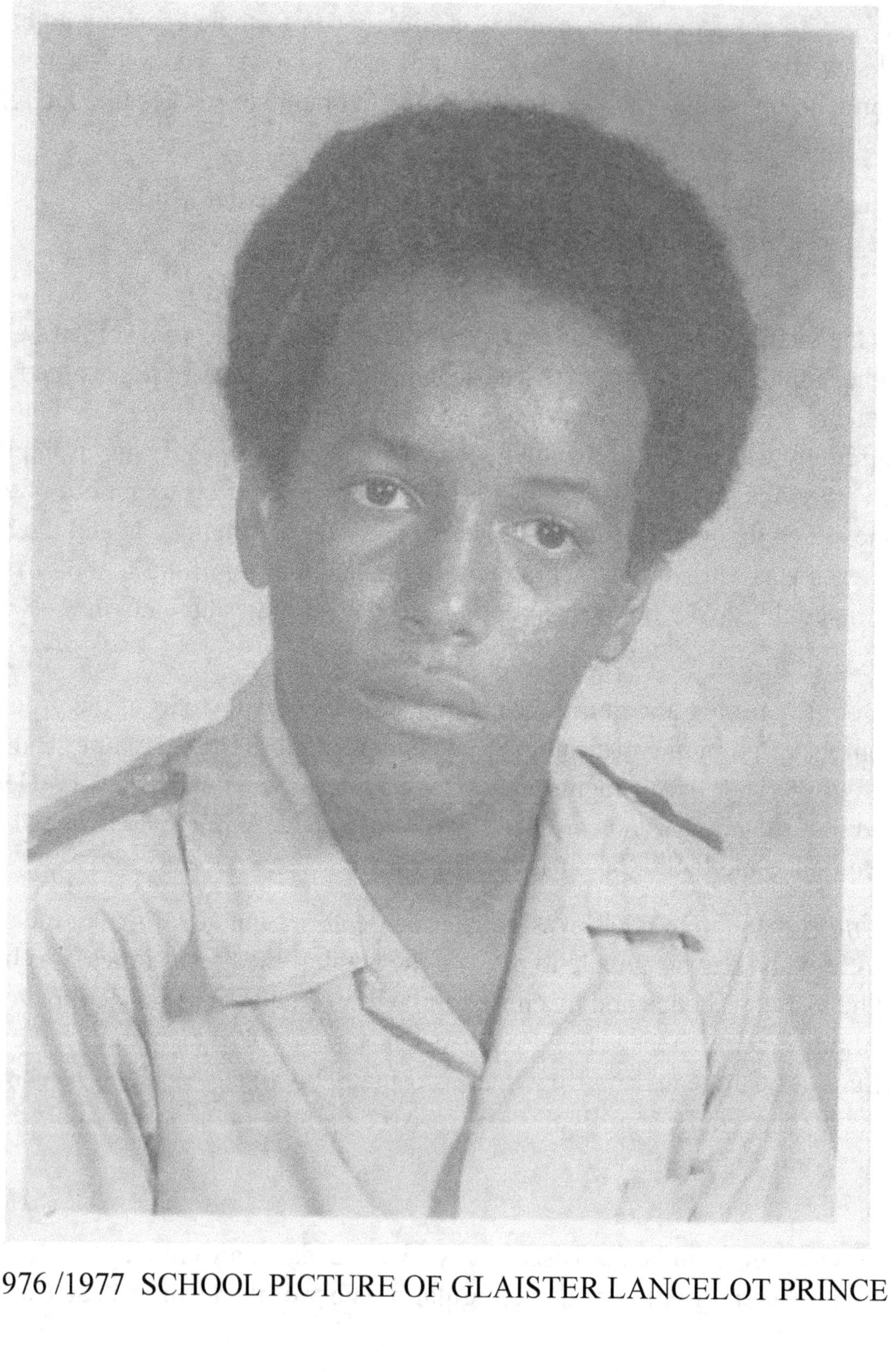

1976 /1977 SCHOOL PICTURE OF GLAISTER LANCELOT PRINCE

CHAPTER 5

1977 – FLIRTING WITH SUCCESS – THE RIGHT MINDSET

In 1977 we reached the Colts cricket finals against TIVOLI GARDEN COMPREHENSIVE HIGH SCHOOL. It was the first time that our school had reached the finals of any competition and it was a significant milestone in our school history. In the sports arena up until that year we were the laughing stock and the beating stick for other schools in the Kingston and St Andrew area. Reaching the finals of any competition takes a lot of hard work and talent and BECKY had guided us to a position where we had the opportunity to compete for the ultimate prize and began to lose the reputation of being the underdog and being the laughing stock.

It would take the arrival of Michael THE DREAD or RED DREAD Hare in 1978 to help put in place the final piece of the puzzle that helped us to have the success that we had. In 1977 we never had the right MINDSET to compete against TIVOLI GARDENS and we were bundled out for a paltry 46 runs and they won without missing a beat.

Speaking to BECKY almost 40 years later he thought we lost because our captain CRACKING did not listen to his advice and play straight when he was batting . He may have been right about CRACKING's lack of discipline and focus when batting but I think we as a team were overawed by the occasion just to be in the finals. Our opponents were the complete opposite they had a " take no prisoners " mentality and were taught to believe they could defeat any team they played especially those uptown upstarts from MEADOWBROOK.

They were MENTALLY a very tough team and their body language displayed that confidence even before the match started , whereas we displayed the nervousness of being in the finals for the first time. Thanks to Wayne "froggy" Fuller who reminded me that our effort would have been more competitive but for the fact that our most consistent batsman as we neared the final , had dengue fever and did not play in the finals. This must have adversely affected our performance that day.

MEADOWBROOK HIGH SCHOOL 1977 COLTS CRICKET TEAM FINALIST

Seated right to left

Douglas Crooks , Glaister Prince, Sean Munroe, Glen Atkins(captain), Kingsley Barnes , Lenworth Johnson, Christopher Fisher , Lloyd Wayne Campbell.

Standing left to right

Mr. Griffith , Richard Chung , Ian Chung, Wayne Fuller ,Andrew Boxer , Courtney Strudwick , Donat Dixon , Carl Harris , Ferdinand Bent , Neville Beckford .

At the time TIVOLI GARDEN had the reputation of being one of the toughest communities in Jamaica. It was the political stronghold of the JLP (Jamaica Labour Party), the opposition party in the 70"s . Before it was TIVOLI GARDEN it was " back o wall" the city dump. Edward Seaga the (JLP leader) at the time had turned that dump into TIVOLI GARDEN and it became a fortress and the epicenter of the JLP. JAMAICA in the late 1970 's had become a battleground for the hostilities resembled the ' cold war ' fought between the two superpowers of the world at the time, the USA and SOVIET UNION.

The prime minister Michael Manley was flirting with taking our country to a situation that would make Jamaica, another CUBA and the USA did not intend to make the same mistake they made with CUBA in the 1960's . They behind the scenes favored the lesser of the extremes Mr. Seaga as their man in Jamaica. There was an increase in violence to protect political turf and the inhabitants of Tivoli were prepared for the struggle which was avoided by the people's vote.

This was the community that our opponents came from and looking back it is no surprise to me that those players came into that match MENTALITY tougher and more prepared to win than we were at MEADOWBROOK. They were literally fighting for their survival from their political opponents the (PNP People National Party), the ruling government party. The fact is that our team went into that final as just another match and our opponents were coming from a background where losing was understood as a matter of life and death. We never stood a chance and even though the match was played on neutral ground (Kensington cricket club in east Kingston) they were mentally ready for battle and we were not.

Later I experienced 2 examples of the toughness and militancy that was synonymous with TIVOLI GARDEN, and looking back at when we eventually won our first trophy in 1982, it was only after we defeated TIVOLI GARDEN in a match that I felt we were mentally prepared to win. One year we were playing a Sunlight Cup match against them at their school ground and were putting up a reasonably creditable performance. During the match a ' gentleman' circled the cricket field and began shouting to the umpire " do a thing now". Shortly after that some very dubious decisions were given against us and even the "impartial " umpires were intimidated by TIVOLI GARDEN. The next time was 1988 after Hurricane Gilbert and the JLP was the government.

My father had made a connection to purchase some zinc at a " discounted" price from someone in TIVOLI GARDENS. Working at JBC IN THE 1980S my father worked with a lot of people from TIVOLI GARDENS. However, I soon discovered the fortress that it had reputed to be from way back in 1977 when I realized I had to be escorted into and out of the community and road blocks had to be removed to enter and leave the community. I did get my zinc, but I left realizing that TIVOLI GARDENS was in so far as its residents were concerned, a state within a state, much like the VATICAN city in ROME.

Having the right MINDSET was an attitude illustrated to me by the great WEST INDIES cricket team of the 70S and 80s. When that team played they knew that it was more than just cricket and more than any player during that era VIV RICHARDS epitomizes the mental toughness when he was batting and when he became captain. In one unfortunate statement his countryman from ANTIGUA who became captain after him had commented in the first match that WEST INDIES played SOUTH AFRICA (after being readmitted back into the international community) in which WEST INDIES lost that it was just another match. He clearly had not read CLR JAMES (Beyond the Boundary) and realized the significance of a black WEST INDIES cricket team being defeated by an almost all- white SOUTH AFRICAN team and described it as " just another match".

When Mr. Hare arrived to be sportmaster at MEADOWBROOK in 1978, the final piece of the puzzle was being put in place because he was the one mainly responsible to create a culture of MENTAL TOUGHNESS, which he called the KILLER INSTINCT and because of our team was very successful in the years going forward and until he left in 1986.

CHAPTER 6

FINALLY MAKING THE TEAM – 1977 –OUR FIRST SCENT OF SUCCESS

In 1977 in my third year in high school I finally was able to become a regular member of the colts cricket team. This I think was mainly due to the fact that we now had a coach who selected his team based purely on merit. Mr. Neville "BECKY Beckford was our chemistry teacher who stumbled into the job of being our colts cricket coach in 1977 and his guidance and skill in spotting and nurturing talent played an integral role in our success on the cricket field over the next 10 years. When Christopher Cheddar and I spoke to him on the phone in early 2017 he told us that he had no idea that he would end up coaching our team. He told us that when Mr. Warren Thorpe (the Bajan born principal of Meadowbrook between 1970-1979) heard that he had played some cricket for the UWI, Mr. Thorpe asked him if he could help the team .

He accepted the offer. The team was then being picked on merit and not based on the friendship of the senior players on the team. This subtle and almost innocuous change instituted by "BECKY" was critical in allowing unknown talent to blossom and flourish. This would not occurred were there a policy not based on merit selection. This policy of merit selection was also important to the success of the greatest and most dominating black sports team ever assembled that was the WEST INDIES cricket team under the captaincy of Clive Lloyd and Vivian Richards in the 1970s and 1980s. They went literally undefeated for 15 years and that dominance made WEST INDIAN communities proud for a generation.

I also think this policy of merit selection was an important part of the REGGAE BOYS making it to the world cup in 1998. The coach RENE SIMONES also picked his team on merit and not who knew who, as was done in the past.

This colts team included GLEN ATKINS , DOUGLAS CROOKS , LENWORTH "JAGO" JOHNSON, CHRISTOPHER FISHER , COURTNEY STRUDWICK, WAYNE FULLER , LLOYD "BEENEY" CAMPBELL ,SEAN MUNROE KINGSLEY BARNES , IAN CHUNG, RICHARD CHUNG, ANDREW BOXER, DONAT DIXON, CARL HARRIS, FERDINAND BENT.

The first official match that year was against St Georges College on north street where this school was located. One of the wonderful memories I had from

playing cricket was visiting so many different schools in Kingston and St Andrew initially and eventually all over Jamaica. Had I not been playing cricket I would never have had the opportunity of knowing so many different communities all over Jamaica. The field at St George's College was strategically located to see SABINA PARK (the home of test cricket in Jamaica) and it was the first time I had seen SABINA PARK. Even though it was before the massive GEORGE HEADLEY STAND was built I was in awe to finally view a famous cricket ground from up close. Later that year in April of 1977 I finally went to see my first test match at SABINA PARK where the WEST INDIES played PAKISTAN (the most talented team to challenge the WEST INDIES team on the first day of that test match. I didn't even know how to get to SABINA PARK on my own, so I had to ask for directions from 'BECKY' who told me to take a bus to Cross Roads roads and walk down south camp road until you see a big white wall on the right.

My father who worked at JBC(JAMAICA BROADCASTING CORPORATION) at the time had made arrangements for me to meet a member of the camera crew who would get me into the match as part of their crew. (JBC was the only Local TV station at the time). My father's friend DAWKINS got me into the match and I stood beside the camera crew all day to see GORDON GREENIDGE make an even 100 with some square cuts and cover drives I had never seen before.: IMRAN KHAN taking 6 wickets with movement and pace, ANDY ROBERTS bowling SADIQ MOHAMMAD with a well disguised slower ball and the athleticism in the field from VIVIAN RICHARDS and ALVIN KALLICHARAN. These were the cricketers I had read about and heard described on cricket commentary ever since I fell in love with playing, reading and watching cricket. The opportunity to see a cricket match live between the best players in the world for the first time was a memory that has never left me.

In our first match against St Georges, I was the opening batsman and the St Georges opening bowler was CARTER. The first ball he bowled to me was pitched outside the off - stump and moved slightly away, but the pace was not as fast as anything "CRACKING' had ever bowled to me so even though butterflies were in my stomach from just being on the pitch, batting his pace was something I felt I could negotiate and survive.

The second ball did the same thing -pitch outside the off stump which I left alone and it went slightly away from me to the wicketkeeper. The third ball was pitched in the same place and I proceeded to leave it alone and was deceived when the ball moved in the other direction and I was bowled for a "DUCKS' (for Zero).

I was disappointed and felt dejected for letting down the team . Fortunately JAGO who batted at #4 later came in and made a gritty 37 and we were able to put up a respectable and competitive score. It was the first time I had seen a fast bowler move the ball the way a spin bowler turned the ball. BECKY never dropped me from the team even after such an inauspicious beginning and when we played TIVOLI GARDENS in the finals later that year I was still a member of the team.

CHAPTER 7

1978 – CAPTAINCY AND MR. MICHAEL HARE (AKA – THE DREAD)

In 1978, I was made captain of the colts cricket team by BECKY and THE DREAD became sportsmaster at MEADOWBROOK. Although THE DREAD never coached the colts team at the time, he along with BECKY worked closely together with and began instituting one program for all the teams that represented MEADOWBROOK in any cricket competition. They along with a former student who was now teaching at MEADOWBROOK (GERALD "G" BELNAVIS) formed the nucleus of an unofficial selection committee that put the infrastructure, planning and coordination in place which laid the foundation for MEADOWBROOK to dominate school - boy cricket for the next 8 years .

Unknown to me at the time of going to school, they wielded tremendous influence with the principal and the academic staff on players who were given an opportunity to represent MEADOWBROOK because of their cricketing ability. This was customary for the Manning Cup squad, but players like RICHARD "RANNY" EVANS , STAFFORD 'PEG HEAD' DUFFUS, KIRTON EBANKS and his brother DILLION EBANKS were given the opportunity to represent MEADOWBROOK, because of the influence and support of the " selection committee" .

Later that " selection committee' also had influence in encouraging the principal and other academic staff to allow me to repeat 5th form in 1980 and be also allowed to enter 6th form.

The DREAD later in 2017 informed me I an email explaining the foundation of our success that parental support was critical in getting proper infrastructure in place. MR. CHUNG (father of the twins IAN AND RICHARD CHUNG) at his personal expense laid a proper practice concrete pitch on the school grounds which the DREAD had recognized was essential if we were going to improve our competitiveness. The laying of the brand new concrete pitch made two things possible. The first thing was that it caused us to practice more frequently on a proper practice pitch. The concrete pitch that existed before was dangerous and unplayable most of the time. Secondly it facilitated more time for training and

made practicing easier because we did not have to walk 10-25 minutes to get to our main field BOTTOM FIELD to start practicing.

Our school grounds were never big enough to have a proper cricket or football pitch and although BOTTOM FIELD was a wonderful location to play official matches it was a disadvantage to be forced to travel 10-15 minutes every time before we started a training session.

With the pitch in place THE DREAD was able to institute what I now realize and consider the most critical factor for our dominance and success in the years to follow -DELIBERATE PRACTICE. Practicing daily to deliberately improve our skills whether batting bowling or fielding. Any player who did not fall in line with that schedule was literally sidelined. The willingness to practice to deliberately improve your skill , no matter how talented you thought you were, became the most important requirement to make the team.

This was great news for me because knowing my athletic limitations allowed me the opportunity to eventually make the team despite being less talented than most other players, but with deliberate practice, I got better and better and was able to compete with both bat and ball by the time we won our first trophy in 1982. My weight and my inability to run fast limited my success at improving as a fielder. I have always mentioned to friends that if BRIAN LARA came to MEADOWBROOK during that era, I am not sure with a prima donna attitude that he would have made the team.

The DREAD began to build on the foundation that BECKY built with the colts team that made it to the finals in 1977. He adopted the same selection policy that BECKY used successfully in putting together his team , a policy that SINGAPOREANS would describe as meritocratic selection. SINGAPORE is a country in southeast ASIA that is about the size of the PARISH of HANOVER with a population of 5.6 million people. Despite its small size and autocratic rule (for example, you are not allowed to chew gum in SINGAPORE) it is now one of richest countries in the world with a GDP about $US 683 billion compared to JAMAICA'S GDP of about US$29 Billion in 2023, World Economics.

It is rumored that when SINGAPORE got independence in 1965 the leadership visited JAMAICA to see what they could learn from JAMAICA in developing as an independent nation. Other factors clearly played a role and SINGAPORE has a similar climate as JAMAICA, but it is my opinion that the

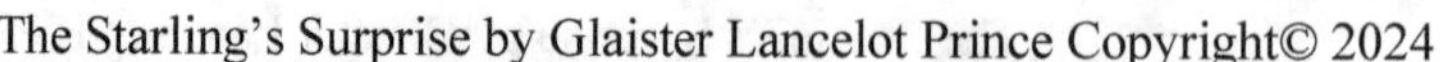

SINGAPORE Goverment's policy of MERITOCRACY has played a significant role in making SINGAPORE one of the most affluent countries today.

We at MEADOWBROOK who played sports during what turned out to be our GOLDEN YEARS were fortunate to be under the guidance of Neville BECKY Beckford and Michael THE DREAD Hare who believed in ameritocratic selection which ensured that new talent was encouraged to blossom and flourish and because of this the best team was always selected. I don't think I would have been given the opportunity to play competitively for our school had some less meritorious system prevail.

This selection process was foundational to the system which the DREAD used : a series of different cricket and football competitions throughout the school, (e.g. form , inter-house, six a side cricket and football tournaments throughout the school. We entered into various competitions which we had never entered before. As we improved , we first won a major contest in 1982 and continued winning until 1986. By then we were playing a cricket match virtually every weekend and sometimes against teams who were older and much more experienced than we were.

These matches allowed us to improve our skills and gave us the opportunity to continue a process of DELIBERATE PRACTICE which played a key role in our school success.

CHAPTER 8

1979 – FINALLY MAKING THE SUNLIGHT CUP SQUAD

In 1979 in my first year at fifth form I became a regular member of the SUNLIGHT CUP SQUAD, played infrequently in the SUNLIGHT CUP matches, but was given an opportunity to improve and test my skill by playing in either a MINOR CUP or EVELYN CUP match. By this time MEADOWBROOK had produced great individual sports performances at ISSA BOYS CHAMPS. HOWARD THOMAS had won the class 3 ,100 meters ; JEFFERY WALTERS had won the class 2 ,400 meters and DONAT " STALLION or STALLI " MAIR had won the class 1, 400 and 800 meters. STALLI went on to represent JAMAICA at the JUNIOR CARIFTA GAMES.

It made our school proud but we still had not won a TEAM competition. Winning a team competition galvanizes and inspires a greater number of people and is much more difficult to achieve because it means getting at least 11 players to play for each other and themselves. The success of the REGGAE BOYS in qualifying for the World Cup in FRANCE in 1998 is a good example of what needs to be done to get any sports team to be successful .

JAMAICA has had a great legacy in individual track and field competition since the 1948 LONDON Olympics where HERB MCKENLEY, DR AUTHUR WINT, LES LAING AND GEORGE RHODEN, broke through on the world track and field scene. This tradition has continued and improved throughout the years with the performance of DONALD QUARRIE at the 1976 MONTREAL Olympics, MERLENE OTTEY at various Olympics and more recently as a country we still continue to produce top class athletes like USAIN BOLT.

Our achievement is so significant that I think on a per capita basis JAMAICA has produced the best track and field performance worldwide since the 1948 LONDON Olympics. However in an individual sport MERIT is relatively easy to identify and talented individuals who DELIBERATELY practice to improve their skill can become world class athletes by performing better than their competitors.

So THE DREAD proceeded to introduce a well regimented and structured yearlong training program that allowed all the teams he coached to enhance their skill and talent by practicing DELIBERATELY. We started training during the summer holidays with strength and weightlifting and long distance running to improve our stamina. We also spent a lot of time in fielding practice (many players were able to make the team solely because of their excellence on the field).

He made us appreciate the value of players who were able to save 20 or 30 runs in the field and how their ability to pull off a stunning catch or remarkable run -out always had the effect of lifting the morale of the team to greater heights. It also ensured that other teammates whose fielding was never up to these excellent standards (like myself) improved by this regimen of DELIBERATE practice and were also motivated by these players' brilliance in the field. Looking back, this was a shrewd strategy which gave us an edge in many close matches that we won.

Bowlers also went through a training regimen where they would practice for hours of just pitching the ball at a particular length aiming at one stump with no batsman batting. This process created and improved many hidden talents in those who had never played cricket before. Stanford GOOSEY Brown admitted to me almost 35 years after our memorable 1982 victory that he came to MEADOWBROOK to play football and he had never played cricket before and it was this training regimen that gave him the impetus to become a competent medium fast bowler and our top wicket -taker in the finals against CALABAR.

DELIBERATE PRACTICE allows the teams to experience small consistent improvement. This is far more important than a culture of rushing to achieve perfection before investing in the training. This is illustrated when the LAKERS' coach PAT RILEY introduced a system called the CBE (career best effort). The LAKERS in 1985 were considered the most talented basketball team ever assembled at the time but were defeated in the western conference finals. RILEY devised a plan and challenged his team using a matrix to track their individual performance and implored each team member for a 1% improvement over his individual performance over the previous year. He thought that if each team member could improve his individual performance by just 1% the result for the team would be exponential and trophies would follow. The result was that the LAKERS won back to back NBA titles, the first team in 20 years to achieve this feat.

I am not sure if the DREAD or BECKY actually devised a matrix to track our performances, but every team member in all those teams gradually got better

with consistent DELIBERATE PRACTICE. It is clear that the successes were a result of our policy of measured improvement. However before we started winning trophies we had to get what I consider the most important aspect of the process in place, our MINDSET.

When we did reach the semifinals of the SUNLIGHT CUP our unprepared mindset was exposed and the result was as embarrassing as we experienced in the colts final against TIVOLI GARDENS in 1977.

CHAPTER 9

1980 – GETTING REGULAR PLAYING TIME AND MENTAL   TOUGHNESS

In 1980 I finally became a team member who got to play most of the matches. I played most games in the 1980 season, where I batted anywhere between #1, all the way to # 7. This was the year I repeated fifth form and we made it to the semi-final against a powerful KINGSTON COLLEGE (KC) team . It was the first time we had got that far in any senior school boy sports competition and our hard work and DELIBERATE PRACTICE were beginning to pay off because our team had come a far way and we were no longer the "beating stick " of other schools. The fact is however that many of the players from that KC went on to represent JAMAICA and the WEST INDIES senior team whereas our mental toughness was found wanting and we put up a score that was uncompetitive .

The team captained by ALFRED "HITCHCOCK" HENRY included DOUGLAS CROOKS , GLEN ATKINS and a very talented little batsman by the name of DEBON or DEVON "DANGO' HINES. DANGO was a very small player barely over 5 feet tall but with a cricket bat in his hands he had supreme ability and played all the strokes in the cricket book. His stroke playing was backed up by his chattering especially when he was at the crease batting whether in training or in any official match. He played the fast bowling of CRACKING with impunity in training sessions and was equally at home against spin bowling and when he got going in a match he provided the players on the field especially the bowlers a running commentary of his audacious stroke play.

I remember one Sunday afternoon in a MINOR CUP match against CITY TREASURY , he and I batted together for over 2 hours and he dispatched all the bowlers to the boundary with ease and I only made 23 because he was in such good form that I was only interested in rotating the strike to allow him the opportunity to continue his magnificent performance. It was this match that showed me the importance of partnership in team sports because even though I only made 23 when DANGO and I were together at the crease batting our partnership netted over 100 runs.

This lesson was very important and when I became captain of the team in 1981 and 1982 I used that same strategy with great success because I recognized that most of the other batsmen were far more talented but if I stayed at the crease batting with them and constantly encouraging them at the end of every over to focus on the prize and curb their natural stroke playing ,we could put up a competitive score.

However, despite having the talent to compete against KC in 1980 , our entire batting line - up again crumbled under the mental pressure of a semi-final challenge and we were bundled out for less than 100. Most opponents would not lose if they bowled out their opposition for under 100 runs and KC won by 10 wickets. I was very disappointed, not because we lost but because we lost without competing and the following year the DREAD started talking about getting our mindset right for the big occasion.

	O	M	R	W			
Williams	18	1	78	1	Total 101	H. Clarke c Anderson b Shaw 5
McKenzie	18	4	69	1	Wickets fell at: 3, 15, 50, 57, 56, 57, 65, 91, 96.	A. Brown c Levy b

Easy win for KC

Defending Sunlight cup Schoolboys cricket champions Kingston College easily gained a place in the final of the competition when they defeated Meadowbrook High School by ten wickets at Clan Carthy yesterday afternoon.

Kingston College were led by three good performances from their top players. Skipper Marlon Tucker captured four for 14, leg spinner Robert Haynes five for 39 and opening batsman Wayne Lewis hit an undefeated 57.

Meadowbrook High School who had first strike started badly losing a wicket with eight runs on the board. However, they managed to hold out for a brief period before spinners Tucker and Haynes had them out for 81 runs. Only Glen Atkins with 28 not out (four fours and a six), D. Hinds 20 (two fours) showed any fight. The wickets fell at 8, 57, 45, 52, 52, 69, 70, 75, 81, 81.

Tucker's figures were 15-6-14-4 while Haynes' were 14.5 — 5 — 39 — 5.

Kingston College in their reply took little time to get the total needed for victory with openers Wayne Lewis and Mark Johnson hitting off the score without being separated. Lewis who made 57, hit seven fours and one six, while Johnson got 26.

The game ended at 5.32 p.m.

Juniors steal the show
at Liguanea

MEADOWBROOK HIGH SCHOOL DEFEATED BY KC

The DREAD called it 'KILLER INSTINCT' but getting your mindset right might be the most important process which makes individual athletes, teams or corporations successful at the highest level. Getting the right mindset is very difficult to pinpoint until you finally get it because like the famous quote from a Supreme Court Justice in the USA, POTTER STEWART "I'LL KNOW IT WHEN I SEE IT' (in his attempt to define certain taboo subjects in a1964 Case.)

MINDSET is like that you cannot necessarily describe it, but you certainly know it when you see it. MINDSET is one of the big differences between USAIN BOLT and his competition and it gives an athletes an aura of invincibility. The WEST INDIES cricket team of the 1980s had that MENTAL TOUGHNESS.

Unfortunately our team had not yet acquired this KILLER INSTINCT and we crumbled against a team and a school which has a long tradition of excelling on the field of sport. (KC won the boys' championship for 15 consecutive years in the 1960s and 1970s) .

So just like the COLTS final against TIVOLI GARDEN in 1977 we had worked hard to reach the semifinal of a schoolboy competition and we had not put up a competitive score , and we surrendered far too easily. It seemed as if our team was in a state of "shellshock" by just being in a semi –final. Talent -wise we were good enough to reach so far in the competition but we were unprepared mentally as a team and for the next 2 seasons THE DREAD talked about us acquiring this KILLER INSTINCT more and more until it became part of our DNA and MEADOWBROOK won several competitions over the next 6 years.

However the next season we lost most of the team members who played in the 1980 semi –final and the DREAD set about picking his squad from a nucleus of younger players to rebuild the talent lost with the exodus of senior players.

CHAPTER 10

1981 – CAPTAINCY

With the exodus of the majority of the players from the 1980 squad , the first task at the start of the 1981 season was to assign a captain for the team. It was a choice between LENWORTH "JAGO' JOHNSON, LLOYD or WAYNE "BEENEY' CAMPBELL and myself. JAGO and BEENEY had one more year left in sixth form and were more senior players than I on the Sunlight Cup team. I thought one of the two would be appointed captain and the other vice-captains.

I was pleasantly surprised when I was appointed captain of the team . THE DREAD , BECKY AND G (GERALD BELVANIS) had campaigned very hard behind the scene for me to be given the opportunity to enter sixth form and the principal McLennon (SPANNA) relented and I entered sixth form in 1981.

In the first match against CAMPERDOWN , I was a bit unsure and nervous about leading the team as I thought either JAGO or BEENEY were more deserving of appointment as captain. Fortunately that first match as captain I played my most stroke filled innings as a competitive cricketer and the butterflies in my stomach went away and from that match going forward I assumed the role of leading the team without any nervousness or lack of confidence.

Normally whenever I bat I graft and build an innings with lots of singles and partnership ,but in that first match against CAMPERDOWN , everything seemed to click and every ball seemed to strike the middle of the bat and I played all the strokes in the book. By the time I reached 50, I had struck 11 or 12 (fours) and I eventually made 88. It was the closest I came to making a century in any competitive match and it was the most entertaining innings I have ever played.

My confidence grew and I was comfortable in my role as the leader of the team . More importantly the rest of the team saw me as a capable Captain . Even though that 1981 sunlight cup team was a young team, (since we had lost most of our senior players from the 1980 team that made it to the semi- finals), we missed making it to the semi- finals by only one point.

.

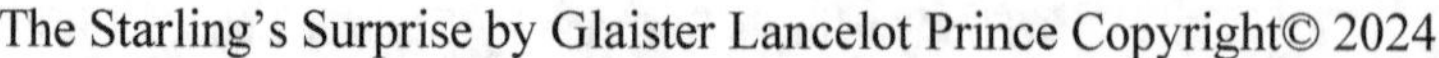

The DREAD used the year as a rebuilding process and he spoke more and more to us about getting our KILLER INSTINCT right.

After the disappointment in the 1980 sunlight cup semi-final , where we surrendered without putting up a fight , the DREAD talked about getting our mindset right from our first blackboard / classroom training session. During the season on match day he would constantly remind us whether we were batting , bowling or fielding of what we spoke about in our classroom training secession by simply shouting out our name and pointing to his head meaning that we should get our MINDSET RIGHT. He did not want any of us to be slipping or lapsing into mediocrity.

He knew that we had the talent to compete at the highest level (our practice and training regimen had made sure that we were well prepared) but he also knew if we did not get our MINDSET right we would never be successful.

When I first entered MEADOWBROOK in 1974, we never had a good selection process and we never practiced consistently to ensure improvement to be competitive. We played a lot of matches where it seemed as if we knew our opponents were better than ourselves and became satisfied with just playing with an attitude of "we cannot win this match" even before the match started.

Even after we had a good selection process in place and had trained relentlessly to improve our game to be competitive ,we still entered crucial matches (especially against schools with a longer history and tradition than MEADOWBROOK)with a defeatist MINDSET. This was no more evident than in the COLTS finals in 1977 when we lost to TIVOLI GARDEN and also in the 1980 Sunlight Cup semifinals when we lost to KC .

We were good enough to get to the finals and semi- finals but we played as if we did not think we deserve to be there and we were overawed and overwhelmed by our opponents. So we spent a lot of time in the 1981 season getting our MINDSET right because our coach knew that this was the critical factor preventing us from winning. The success achieved in the years that followed proved that he was correct, because once our MINDSET shifted and this affected the players including those who played on the COLTS team.

It was our superior MINDSET that made us defeat CALABAR in 1984 after we made a low score of 100 and we bowled them out for 96. It was also seen in the

1986 team which defeated KC in the finals where we took sweet revenge forbour embarrassing semi-final loss against them by bowling them out for 38.

There was one particular match in our 1982 winning season which epitomized the KILLER INSTINCT to win and once that shift happened , the teams that won in 1984 and 1986 played with an aura of invincibility and confidence demonstrating that we were no longer intimidated by any school , no matter their size or the length of their winning history. During this particular period we had shown that we were no longer the "Cinderella" team and had now become a member of an elite group of schools who were to be feared once we entered a cricket match. This KILLER INSTINCT spread to the football team which won the WALKER CUP in 1986.

CHAPTER 11

1982 – THE PINNACLE OF THE GLORY YEARS

GLAISTER LANCELOT PRINCE MEADOWBROOK HIGH SCHOOL (1982)

After missing the semi- final by one point in 1981, we played our first match against J.C (JAMAICA COLLEGE)in our first match of the 1982 season. They had a good team which included JUNIOR HALL who went on to play for the

JAMAICAN SENIOR CRICKET TEAM and JIMMY ADAMS who went on to captain WEST INDIES SENIOR TEAM. JUNIOR HALL was so confident of his ability as a fast bowler that he started with all the fielders behind the batsmen.

CHRISTOPHER CHEDDAR, exemplifies how our team's confidence had grown because in that first over he nonchalantly with very little backlift stroke caressed the ball to the mid-on boundary. The amazing thing about that stroke was that JUNIOR HALL chased in vain all the way to the boundary without success as the stroke was so well timed that the closer he got the faster it went. Today 40 years since that over, a member of our UNION and member of the DREAD selection committee and staff member RORY MCGREGOR will still tell the story about that day when "CHEDDAR MADE JUNIOR HALL RUN ALL THE WAY TO THE BOUNDARY to no avail.. "

That stroke set the tone of the match and we went on to win the match. In another memorable incident our fast bowler STANFORD (GOOSEY) BROWN , ran out a JC batsman who was backing up too far to steal a single. I was fielding at mid–off and I spotted the batsman at the non–striker's end trying to take advantage by leaving his crease before GOOSEY even delivered the ball. I spoke to GOOSEY quietly on his walk back to the bowler's end and told him of the situation . The next ball GOOSEY ran up to bowl, carried his arm over like he was delivering the ball and turned around and promptly ran out the non–striker.

The umpire upheld our appeal, the JC batsmen and team complained that we were unfair but it demonstrated the aggression in our competitive spirit ; we were not going to let any team take advantage of us by stealing a quick single. After the match the DREAD vindicated our decision because he thought it was well within the law and the spirit of the game. The opposing batsman was trying to take outsmart us but he went too far and we spotted his move into dangerous territory and took full advantage of it. It was not like the famous 1981 incident when the AUSTRALIAN bowler TREVOR CHAPPELL was told by his brother and captain of the team to bowl the last ball underarm to prevent the NEW ZEALANDER BRIAN McKECHNIE from hitting the last ball of the over for six. That incident was within the laws of the game but it was not in the spirit of the game.

The next important match I remember that year was against TIVOLI GARDENS COMPREHENSIVE at bottom field. As I explained earlier we were

embarrassed by TIVOLI in the 1977 COLTS FINAL and no matter where we played them they were always going to be a difficult team to beat. This match was going to be a test of our mental toughness or KILLER INSTINCT as the DREAD described it. We batted first and made 106 and this was not going to be an easy total to defend . I remember bowling at one end and keeping it very tight but they were getting closer and closer to our total and I was not taking any wickets. I wanted to take myself off and trY another bowler and the DREAD shouted from beyond the boundary that I should keep bowling.

This was the only time I can remember the DREAD exercising his discretionary power to prevent me from making a bowling change. We eventually won the match by about 10 runs and after the match the DREAD explained to me that it was better to keep the bowling tight in a tight competitive match instead of experimenting with a new bowler who might be loose and easily give away runs . His judgment turned out to be right and it was the match that determined the fate of our season. We played with such confidence that we only lost one match for the rest of the season and that was against CALABAR, in the TAPPIN CUP semifinal and this mainly happened because the CALABAR players blocked GARFIELD MARSTON from taking a single by deliberately blocking his path from running from one end Of the crease to the other and he was run out, I think unfairly.

CALABAR won that match by less than 5 runs and MARSTON was batting with so much confidence that running him out illegally was the only way they could have won. We were furious ,but we took sweet revenge on them in the SUNLIGHT CUP finals later that year and again in the 1984 SUNLIGHT CUP finals when we won by 4 runs.

There were two other important matches I remember on our way to the semifinal against KC (KINGSTON COLLEGE) at their home ground and a TAPPIN CUP quarter finals against XLCR (EXCELSIOR) or should I say COURTNEY WALSH at Melbourne cricket club. KC had embarrassed us in the 1980 semi-finals and they were always going to be a difficult team to beat. They were not as powerful as they had been , but they had a young fast bowler DERRON DIXON (who went on to play for the JAMAICA senior cricket team in the regional tournament) They batted first and we bowled them out for about 120 which would have been a competitive total for us in the past on their home ground. Our self-belief had matured immeasurably and we won with ease , thanks to some aggressive batting mainly from our vice-captain LLOYD (PIGGY) WILLIAMS .

One stroke I remember where he dispatched DIXON with such disdain to the cover boundary that no fielder moved to try and get the ball. That stroke was symptomatic of our confidence and we were beginning to field we could actually win the SUNLIGHT CUP.

In the TAPPIN CUP quarter-finals against XLCR we faced a very quick and angry COURTNEY(CUDDY) WALSH. CUDDY had just been selected to make his debut for the JAMAICAN SENIOR national team and his confidence was very high. He went on to become the first bowler to take 500 wickets in test cricket and I think he is the WEST INDIES top wicket taker with 519 wickets. XLCR batted first and we bowled them out for a small total. When it became our turn to bat, the XLCR team wanted to borrow our wicket keepers gloves because theirs was in a state of disrepair (maybe from trying to stop those thunderbolts CUDDY bowled to them in training) .

Our coach MIKE (THE DREAD) HARE, in his typically combative way, refused their request. CUDDY, already fired up from being selected for the national team that week was even more incensed and proceeded to produce a disconcerting and lethal spell of bowling for which he became known throughout his cricket career.

The first ball he bowled to CHRISTOPHER CHEDDAR had so much pace and venom that it flew over both CHRISTOPHER and the wicketkeeper's head and bounced only once after it was pitched on the way to the boundary. Pretty soon I was at the crease facing WALSH because both CHEDDAR and GARY SIMMS were dismissed fairly cheaply. The first ball he bowled to me reared from a good length towards my throat and I somehow avoided being hit by this 90 mile an hour missile by backing away to the square leg umpire. I don't know how I avoided being hit and seriously hurt (in those days cricket helmets weren't common) and I was not wearing one in the over that he bowled to me and I survived out of luck . I heard years later from CHRISTOPHER CHEDDAR, who was told by DEVON MCDONALD that the DREAD safely from BEYOND THE BOUNDARY was infuriated and was cussing me saying that " JELLY STAND UP AND BAT AND STOP RUNNING AWAY FROM THE BOWLER ' .

However I don't remember the DREAD castigating me from the sidelines and I was sufficiently intimidated from the first ball and was worried about my safety that I was also dismissed very cheaply. Fortunately both LLOYD PIGGY

WILLIAMS and NOEL ALPHANSO CURTIS were never intimidated by WALSH and batted his deliveries with grit and determination and we won fairly easily.

This was the hallmark and strength of our TEAM , as throughout the season we had no real super star. A member of our TEAM always rises to the occasion whether batting bowling or fielding which ensured that we had enough all round strength to pull off a victory. To this day I still boast that I survived an over against COURTNEY WALSH and lived to tell the tale however embarrassing I must have looked backing away to the square leg umpire.

CHAPTER 12

THE SEMI- FINAL AND FINALS

We were now back into the semi –finals and our opponent was a team of unknown talent ST CATHERINE HIGH SCHOOL.

MEADOWBROOK VS. ST. CATHERINE HIGH

The fact that they were unknown made no difference as just being in the semi- final again after 2 years would be a test of our mental toughness. We knew that we had the ability to defeat any team, but I was worried if we were going to crumble and surrender mentally like we did in the COLTS FINAL of 1977 and the SUNLIGHT CUP SEMI FINALS in 1980.

We batted first in a match that was played at LUCAS OVAL in east KINGSTON. The jitters and the nervousness were soon evident and we were quickly struggling at 17 runs and losing 3 wickets when I went out to bat . STANFORD GOOSEY BROWN was already batting and together we steadied the ship until GOOSEY was dismissed for 26 with our total at 60. I was joined by NOEL PHANSO CURTIS and together we put on a very valuable 61 run partnership. PHANSO top scored with 44 and I made 29. The rest of our innings was epitomized by our gritty partnership typical of our TEAM throughout our winning season with the most significant being the last wicket partnership between CLIVE EDDY EDWARDS who made a swashbuckling 39 with 5 (4s) and GARFIELD MARSTON (who went on to captain the winning 1984 SUNLIGHT

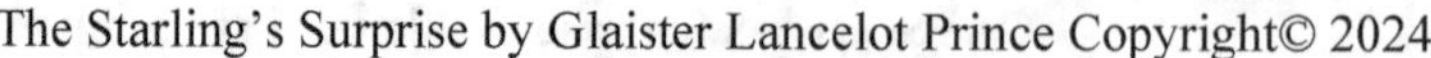

CUP TEAM) who made a typically gritty 14 not out and they put on a valuable 39 runs for the last wicket.

We were eventually bowled out for 195 just 5 runs short of 200 a total we knew we could defend and win on any day. We dismissed them for 69 and won quite easily with PHANSO taking 4 wickets for 12 runs to complete a good all round performance and GRAHAM RHODEN taking 2 wickets for 11 runs and CLIVE EDDY EDWARDS taking 2 wickets for 8 runs to ensure our comfortable victory.

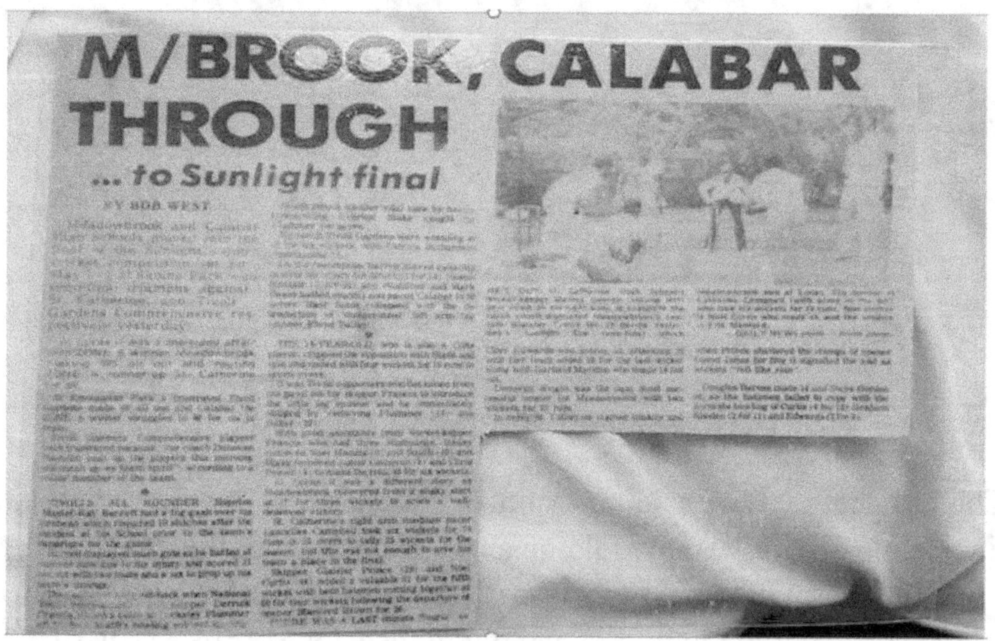

MADE IT TO THE SUNLIGHT CUP FINALS MEADOWBROOK VS. CALABAR

We were now in the SUNLIGHT CUP FINALS for the first time in our school's history and the occasion of just reaching the finals was a significant achievement. No other team from MEADOWBROOK HIGH SCHOOL since it was founded in 1958 had ever reached the final of a premier senior sports competition and the fact that we were to play against CALABAR made the FINALS take on much more significance.

CALABAR was the closest High school to MEADOWBROOK   and had a greater sporting tradition than us. They were responsible for snapping the KINGSTON COLLEGE 15 year reign on BOYS CHAMPS in 1977 and they had won the MANNING CUP and the WALKER CUP. CALABAR had always seen

MEADOWBROOK as an easy school to beat and they had beaten us in the TAPPIN CUP semi–final (by unfair means) so we had a score to settle with them. CALABAR had not won the SUNLIGHT CUP since 1942 despite their great sporting tradition.

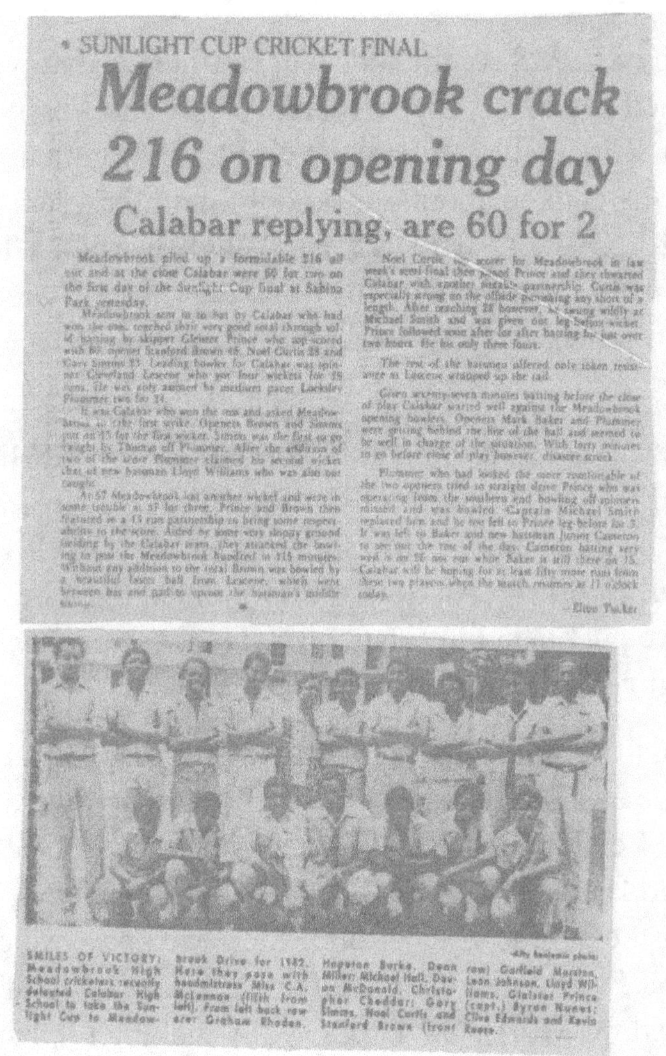

SUNLIGHT CUP CRICKET FINAL

Meadowbrook crack 216 on opening day

Calabar replying, are 60 for 2

SUNLIGHT CUP CRICKET FINAL OPENING DAY

CALABAR won the toss and invited us to bat first . Our opening batsmen SANDFORD GOOSEY BROWN and GARY SIMMS put on a respectable 43 runs for the opening partnership .SIMMS' batting style was as unorthodox as it was pugnacious and a member of our UNION and unofficial MANAGEMENT COMMITTEE GERALD " G" BELVANIS always reminds us of SIMMS first

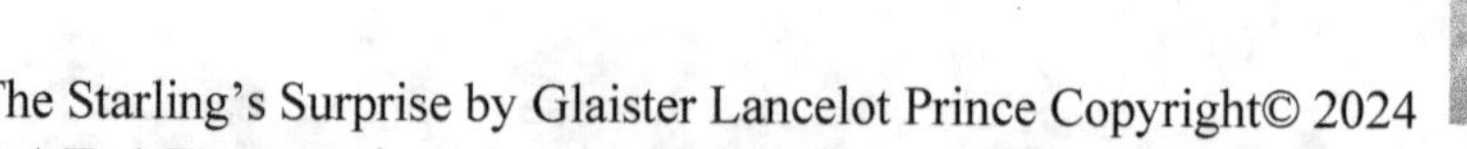

stroke in the match. CALABAR opening bowler and captain MICHAEL SMITH pitched the first ball at full length to SIMMS and in his truly audacious batting style he promptly slapped the ball with such venom back passed the bowler in the air with SMITH hopelessly saying " catch him LECENE" with ball sailing over the CALABAR fielder's head at mid-off that it was in the boundary before he had completed the sentence.

That stroke by SIMMS set the tone and confidence that we had come into the match determined to take revenge on CALABAR and finally shut them up for thinking we were a "Cinderella " school . We had not forgotten all the disrespectful ways they talked about our school for all the years that I attended MEADOWBROOK. NEVILLE BECKY BECKFORD told CHRIS CHEDDAR and I in a phone conversation early in 2017 that the CALABAR coach LES WRIGHT was so confident of victory that they were stunned and dismayed at their comprehensive loss.

However we were soon reeling at 57 for 3 as we lost SIMMS (23) , LLOYD PIGGY WILLIAMS (1) and CHRISTOPHER CHEDDAR for (8) . GOOSEY and I steadied the ship for a valuable partnership of 43 when GOOSEY was dismissed for an invaluable 46. NOEL PHANSO CURTIS joined me when the total was 100 for 4 wickets and we put on an important 66 runs for the fifth wicket partnership with CURTIS making 28.

In a style which became a hallmark of our success we had small but valuable partnerships until we eventually reached over 200 runs and were eventually bowled out for 216. HUGH Leighton GREEN (8) put on 11 runs , CLIVE EDDY EDWARDS (8) and I put on 24 runs, BRYON CANDY NUNES(5) and I put on 7 runs to take us over the psychological total where we knew we could not be beaten. CANDY and I were both dismissed on the same score of 206 and I eventually top scored for MEADOWBROOK, by making 60. I struck only one 4 in that innings , my last match as captain as opposed to the 12 fours I had struck by the time I had reached 50 in my first match as captain in the previous season. GARY MARSTON and GRAHAM RHODEN put on another 10 runs for the last wicket and we were eventually bowled out for 216.

The other members of that historic squad were (HOPETON HITCHY BURKE, DEAN MILLER, MICHAEL T.C HALL, DEVON McDONALD, TIMON WAUGH, LEON JOHNSON and KEVIN REESE).

CALABAR started their reply confidently against our opening bowlers STANFORD GOOSEY BROWN and CLIVE EDDY EDWARDS. They ended the day on 60 runs for 2 wickets after losing LOCKSLEY PEPE PLUMMER and their captain MICHAEL SMITH .

PLAYING TO FINE LEG: Meadowbrook's opener Stanford Brown playing to fine leg off Calabar's captain and medium pacer Michael Smith during his innings of 46 in the Sunlight Cup final a Sabina Park yesterday. The wicketkeeper i Junior Cameron.

Daily News Photo—Charlie Kinkead

PLAYING THE FINE LEG

At 57 Meadowbrook lost another wicket and were in some trouble at 57 for three. Prince and Brown then featured in a 43 run partnership to bring some respectability to the score. Aided by some very sloppy ground fielding by the Calabar team, they attacked the bowling to post the Meadowbrook hundred in 115 minutes. Without any addition to the total Brown was bowled by a beautiful faster ball from Lescene, which went between bat and pad to uproot the batsman's middle stump.

... two openers tried to straight drive Prince who operating from the southern end bowling off-spin missed and was bowled. Captain Michael S... replaced him and he too fell to Prince leg-before f... It was left to Baker and new batsman Junior Cam... to see out the rest of the day. Cameron batting well is on 26 not out while Baker is still there o... Calabar will be hoping for at least fifty more runs ... these two players when the match resumes at 11 o'... today.

— Elton T...

THE TEAM AND MS. McLENNON, PRINCIPAL AT MEADOWBROOK
(1982)

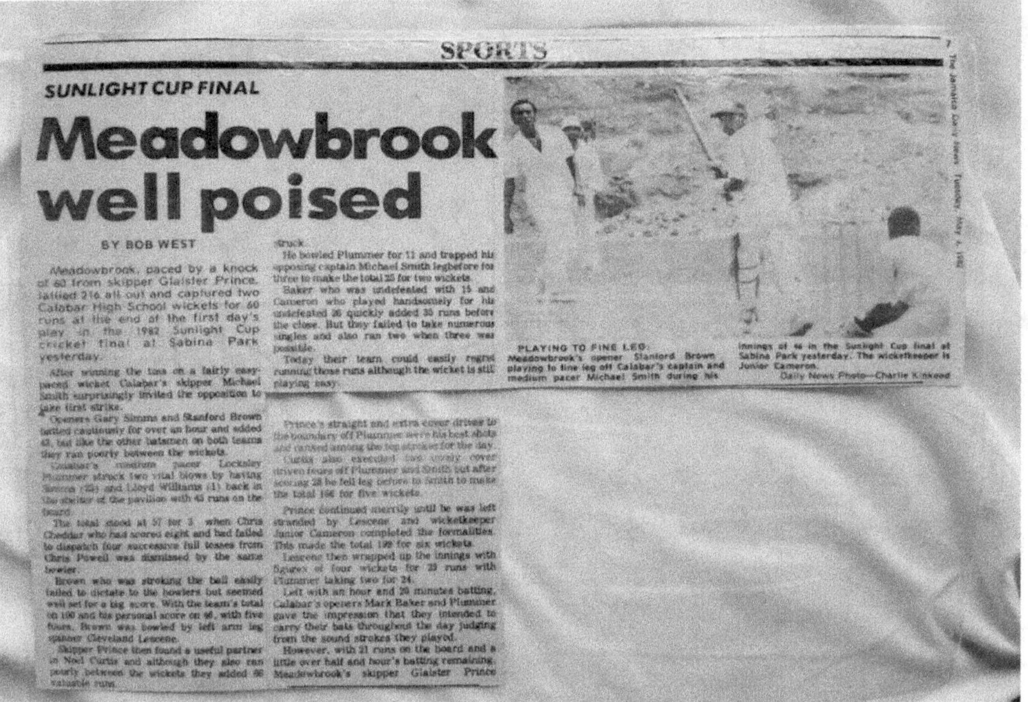

MEADOWBROOK WELL POISED TO WIN

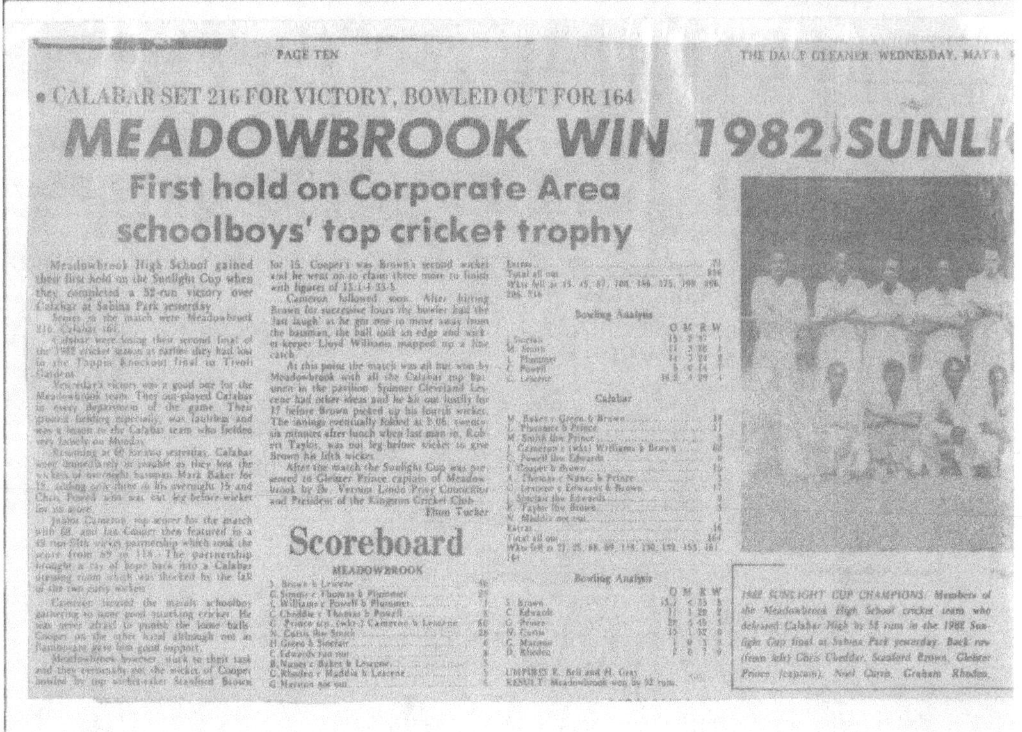

MEADOWBROOK WINS 1982 SUNLIGHT CUP

MEADOWBROOK WINS 1982 SUNLIGHT CUP 'CONTINUED

VICTORY!

The next day JUNIOR CAMERON who top scored in the match with an aggressive 68 took the fight to us, but he had very little support and they were

dismissed for 164 and we won by 52 runs. It was an excellent all- round team performance in the field with CLIVE EDDY EDWARDS taking a stunning catch to dismiss CLIVE LESCENE at mid-off and our wicketkeeper and vice-captain LLOYD PIGGY WILLIAMS taking an equally brilliant catch to dismiss top scorer JUNIOR CAMERON. GOOSEY ended up with a good all round performance by taking 5 wickets for 33 runs from 13 overs , EDDY took 2 for 29 from 11 overs and I took 2 for 45 from 23 overs.

When the last CALABAR batsman was out , our supporters stormed on to the historic SABINA PARK GROUNDS , and I looked up into the sky in praise and thanks for the blessing of being a part of this momentous occasion for our school. We were the pride and joy of our school and our coach THE DREAD and I , in acknowledgement to each other of the significance of the victory, embraced him as we gathered to join in the celebratory victory lap around SABINA PARK track.

In JUNE of 1982 the entire team was honored in a function put on by ESSO STANDARD OIL at bottom field where members of our squad were given a commemorative trophy engraved with our name and the inscription ."1982 SUNLIGHT CUP CHAMPIONS" Whenever I speak to members of the squad , I am told that the miniature Trophy is still part of their cherished memorabilia, 41 years later.

PAGE EIGHT · THE CHILDREN'S OWN · FRIDAY, MAY 14, 1982

Meadowbrook High School win 1982 Sunlight Cup

Meadowbrook High School gained their first hold on the Sunlight Cup when they completed a 52 run victory over Calabar at Sabina Park on Tuesday May 4.

Scores in the match were Meadowbrook 216, Calabar 164.

Calabar were losing their second final of the 1982 cricket season as earlier they had lost in the Tappin Knockout final to Tivoli Gardens.

Tuesday's victory was a good one for the Meadowbrook team. They out-played Calabar in every department of the game. Their ground fielding especially, was faultless and was a lesson to the Calabar team who fielded very loosely on Monday.

Resuming at 50 for two on Tuesday, Calabar were immediately in trouble as they lost the wickets of overnight batsman Mark Baker for 15, adding only three to his overnight 15 and Chris Powell who was out leg before wicket for no score.

Junior Cameron, captaining for the match with 68, and Ian Cooper then featured in a 48 runs fifth wicket partnership which took the score from 69 to 118. The partnership brought a ray of hope back into a Calabar dressing room which was shocked by the fall of the two early wickets.

Cameron treated the mainly schoolboy gathering to some good attacking cricket. He was never afraid to push the loose balls. Cooper on the other hand although not as flamboyant gave him good support.

Meadowbrook however, stuck to their task and they eventually got the wicket of Cooper bowled by top wicket taker Stanford Brown for 35. Cooper was Brown's second wicket and he went on to claim three more to finish with figures of 11.1 4-33-5.

Cameron followed soon. After hitting Brown for successive fours the bowler had the last laugh as he got one to move away from the batsman, the ball took an edge and wicket-keeper Lloyd Williams snapped up a fine catch.

BIG SUNLIGHT CUP CHAMPIONS: Members of the Meadowbrook High School cricket team who defeated Calabar High by 52 runs in the 1982 Sunlight Cup final at Sabina Park on Tuesday, May 4. Back row (from left) Claris Cheddar, Stanford Brown, Glaister Prince (captain), Noel Currie, Graham Rhoden, Michael Hall, Byron Watson, Gary Knott, Kevin Brown and Lloyd Williams (wicket keeper). Stooping from left: Leon Morris, Horston Butler, Byron Nunes, Garfield Marston, Hugh Green, Clive Edwards and Dwayne McDonaId. Missing from picture is coach Michael Hart.

MEADOWBROOK HAS THE CUP: Glaister Prince (right), captain of the Meadowbrook High School Sunlight Cup team proudly presents the cup to his headmistress Miss C. McCannon at the beginning of the school's silver anniversary celebrations with a lunch hour concert. Other members of the team which defeated Calabar High School to win the cup for the first time are in the background.

ESSO HAILS MEADOWBROOK SUNLIGHT VICTORY: Meadowbrook Cricket Captain Glaister Prince (left) receives his Esso Sunlight Champions Captain trophy from Mrs. Pete Fenton, wife of Esso West Indies Refinery Managing...

MEADOWBROOK HIGH SCHOOL WINS 1982 SUNLIGHT CUP

CHAPTER 13
Meadowbrook Golden Years - ESSO connection.

THE MAN, THE MYTH, THE LEGEND GLAISTER LANCELOT PRINCE
WITH THE SUNLIGHT CUP TROPHY AND AWARDS (1982)

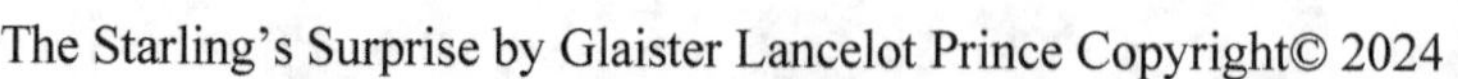

After we created history by being the first team from Meadowbrook High to win a major corporate Area School boy trophy, we were honored and feted at our beloved "Bottom Field". On speaking to my lifelong friend who I met at the function Ramon Gordon; he provided me with the background information to ESSO's connection with Meadowbrook.

Apparently it was Marshall Peterkin who went to school with my sister Claudette (Bibby) who was working at the refinery who made the connection with Meadowbrook once ESSO began searching for somewhere the staff sports club could use as their home-grounds and where they could have regular employee fun days. ESSO built the pavilion in which the special function to honor our Sunlight Cup Team was held.

Ramon told me that it was Dickie Hall and Roy Marshall who did the heavy lifting to organize the function and as he the Public Relations Manager he was just there to introduce the Refinery Manager, Mr. Pete Fenton who handed out the trophies. No expense was spared to make sure the occasion was memorable . My parents (Thomas and Lilly Prince) were also invited guests and Esso treated them like royalty, not because of their name , but because their " baby" was part of the team that put Meadowbrook on the map and they were happy to be there to enjoy the school's historic achievement.

Ramon also handed out a collectors book of the profile of the 1982 FIFA World Cup in Spain which became a cherished possession of all team members and supporters who received a copy.

More importantly ESSO gave all 16 players a trophy for our achievements and after almost 40 years I still have my trophy to remind me of that wonderful year. Another member of that 1982 squad (Kevin Reese who captained the 1986 winning Sunlight Cup team) told me in 2016 that he still has his trophy. On behalf of all 16 members of that team (whether living or who have already transitioned into another world like Lloyd "Piggy " Williams) I want to express my gratitude to those who made our team feel special by the event they organized and the trophies presented.

This history is now documented for all past and future students of Meadowbrook to read and hopefully never to forget those Golden Years between 1982-1986.

CHAPTER 14

EMAIL FROM MR MICHAEL HARE

Email from the Dread in 2016

Hi Jelly,

Your email was certainly a surprise, but good to hear from you anyway. At the time I was heavily involved in a family illness which eventually resulted in death and all the funeral arrangements etc. Then there was Xmas and New Year...- so apologies for taking so long to respond.

I'll try to answer most of your questions...

Came to Jamaica in 1974.

Worked at Rusea's, St. Jago and Turks and Caicos High School before joining Meadowbrook in Sept. 1978.

Hinds vs. Prince for most talented batsman; Hinds for sheer raw talent, but yourself for everything else...- you get the vote...- why?- you made the most of your ability... knew your limitations and worked within them...- if I had to pick someone to score runs to save my life, you would be the one.

Most talented bowler: has to be K. Ebanks...- wonderful natural action... good control of line and length and good use of flight and spin. He would get the nod, but there were many good ones during those years. Incidentally, he would also get my vote for best fielder, - and there again there were many good ones.

Most improved player during my time: Goosie I think, tho Cheddar runs him close. Goosie came to Meadowbrook mainly as a footballer, but he worked hard at his cricket, developed into a fine fast-medium bowler and then into an effective opening bat as well.

Biggest surprise?- there were a few...- the "other" P.Brown's catch off Ebanks in the Sunlight final of 1984 to get rid of Calabar's opening bat...- he was our worst fielder by far and the ball was skied high in his direction with no-one else around to take it instead...- he hovered underneath it and it seemed to take an age to get

down, but he clung on above his head in true "crocodile" fashion. Next morning we bowled them out to win by just 3/4 runs despite only having scored 100 ourselves.

There was also the Spalding Cup final that year against the very highly rated STETHS. To be honest I thought we had no chance and we were easily bowled out for just over 100. They seemed to be cruising, but even I underestimated our spinners and fielding skills and we fought back to only lose by only 1 wicket...- That was a surprise and I was very proud of the team that day (as on many other occasions). Also in the 1986 Sunlight final, K.C. disintegrating from 38/0 to 58 all out on a rain affected wicket was a big shock...- fantastic bowling that morning from Ebanks and Hopeton Burke.

Other special memories: well we made some good progress with the football team as well, though not to the same extent. The Colts team with the 2 Smith twins and Witter and Moore etc. did really well one season, losing only 0-1 to a very strong K.C. side in the final. And the Manning Cup team made steady progress over the years as well.

Factors that led to our Sunlight Cup successes during that period: Discipline, Hard Work, Team Spirit, a great supportive Management Team (Beckie, G., Rory, and later yourself and Beanie and Jago once you'd all left school). Planning, often in great detail, and trying to stay 2/3 steps ahead of the present...- And equipment: I tried to implement a policy of gradually building up good quality gear,- and looking after it while adding more as finances would allow...- the concrete practice pitch installed by Mr. Chung on top field made a great difference as it was not often our clay pitch was good enough to permit quality practice.

Advice to Goosie would be along the same lines...- hard work... stay ahead with the planning and know your long-term and short-term aims... discipline and team spirit go together for me,- hence player involvement for pitch preparations and dropping so-called "stars" if necessary to make a point to one and all. Build from the bottom,- when I first arrived I knew there would be limitations to what could be achieved with an already established Sunlight team, so I worked hard on both

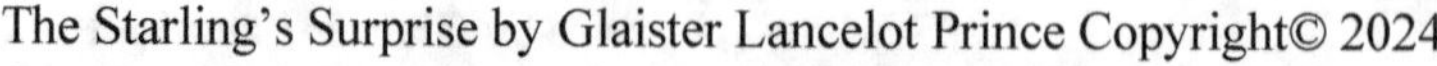

Colts and Junior Colts players and integrated them with the Sunlight squad as soon as it was feasible. And equipment: get the best and look after it.

Other matters: as I recall Jelly certainly beat Paul Brown on that sprint,- over a full 100 meters I think (but I wouldn't swear to it).

And to close, a little indulgence...- my Best Team drawn from the players that represented Meadowbrook during my time there:

1. S.Brown.
2. K.Ebanks.
3. Hinds (what was his 1st name?).
4. C.Cheddar.
5. G.Prince (captain).
6. R.Evans.
7. K.Reece.
8. C.Facey (wk).
9. Paul Smith.
10. H.Burke.
11. P.Brown (now retired Major I understand).

Can't believe I'm not including either Dewar or MacDonald who did so much for the team on so many occasions. Perhaps Dewar for Smith, but this team is not fantastic in the field and we could do wid his athleticism. Other " near misses": "Piggy" Williams, a real competitor who would make runs as well as. keeperwicket,- but Facey is the superior keeper and who else would say a prayer before we started...- also Clive Edwards, a real stalwart and team man (but not as dangerous wid the new ball as Burke). Hinds is a luxury and only included cos you would be captain and could sit on his bullshit when necessary.

Well that's it. It's been interesting and given me an enjoyable hour or so reflecting on the past.

Hope all is ok with you. I've just about finished wid even part-time work now and spend a bit more time on the golf course (frustrating game!). Take care now, Mike.--
On Wed, 23/11/16, Glaister Prince <glaisterp@gmail.com> wrote:
Subject: Meadowbrook golden years

CHAPTER 15

MR. HARE GREATEST LEGACY - ALFRED HITCHCOCK HENRY

**** This chapter is written where I use Hitchcock or Freddy to describe Alfred Henry and The DREAD or MR. Hare to describe Mike Hare (COACH) . This was the friendly way we sometimes refer to each other in the way they both would refer to me as JELLY.

This chapter was written more than 4 years after I had completed the rest of this book in August 2017 .

I had wanted to know more about Mr. Hare (The Dread) and what was his formula to create a successful cricket dynasty at Meadowbrook in such a short time after he came to Meadowbrook in 1978 . When he left in 1986 Meadowbrook had won 3 Sunlight Cup, 2 Tappin Cup and one Walker Cup (football).

This chapter was done after a long 4 hour interview with " Hitchcock" in 2021 and we discussed his relationship with the dread and the success template he got from the Dread which he took to Jamaica College (JC) which inspired JC to win their first manning cup trophy since 1974 (the year I started Meadowbrook) and winning their first triple crown in their football history under the guidance of Hitchcock, Mr. Hare protege.

Hitchcock came to Meadowbrook in 1977 along with his younger brother James "Jim Roy" "bubu Roy" Henry (a Meadowbrook legend in his own right). "Jim Roy" bow legged and much slower than Camperdown and Arnette Garden speedy left winger Errol Blake (Blakey) who made the mistake once too often to embarrass Jim Roy in a manning cup match at the national stadium and Jim Roy tackle left Blakey on the cycle track at the national stadium.

Hitchcock was born and grew up in Marverly (a community that shares the border with Pembroke Hall.)

He went to Marverly All Age upon not getting into a traditional High School, he persuaded his parents to send him to a private High School (Grantham High School located in Cross Roads.

 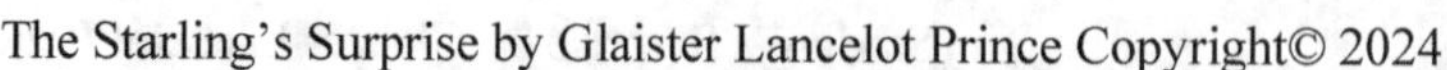

At Grantham he connected with a well-known Pembroke Hall name who was also at Grantham at the time (Stylistic) and Hitchcock made Pembroke Hall his second home after Stylistic introduced him to the other footballers in Pembroke Hall, especially the ballers from Potosi Rovers who he still has lifelong friendships with.

He was brought to Meadowbrook by then Meadowbrook coach Devon Jeffrey (former Jamaica and Santos Footballer who also played for Asphalt Football Club in the Pembroke Hall Corner (the best Corner in Jamaica in the early 1970s.)

Devon was impressed by Hitchcock's maturity at a practice match he was goalkeeping and was wondering who was this "Likkle Bwoy " shouting out instructions to him while he was playing Center Half. The match was arranged by "Phut" (the coach who took Meadowbrook to their only football trophy in 1985 (the Walker Cup).

Hitchcock's loyalty and relationship with "Putt" went way back since Putt invited Hitchcock (a school boy) to sign on the committee that was instrumental in the formation of Marverly Football Club . When the Dread was no longer interested in coaching 1985. Meadowbrook football team Hitchcock was instrumental in getting "Putt" the opportunity to coach Meadowbrook.

Hitchcock met the DREAD in 1978 , and the DREAD used to watch Hitchcock in the manning cup training . The Dread admired Hitchcock's maturity with his interaction with the other team members and invited him to come to Sunlight training . Hitchcock was unable to make the Sunlight training since the Sunlight training began in the summer that manning cup training was going on in the summer . (The Dread started his coaching regime in the summer before the Sunlight season began in January every year).

After seeing Freddy and Jago organize and inspire a group of first formers to play senior house cricket for Saunders (which they won that year) the DREAD appointed Freddy as captain of the 1980 Sunlight Cup team which reached the semi -final . This was an historic moment in our school because Meadowbrook had never reached the semi- final of the 2 most important team sports in Jamaica high school competition (football (soccer) or cricket).

Our performance was disappointing but the groundwork was being laid for the success that came at Meadowbrook and Freddy's inspirational legacy at JC(Jamaica College).

In 1981 Freddy started working with the help of Mrs. Chung (Richard and Ian Chung mother who were members of that 1980 Sunlight Cup team that made the semi -finals) who helped him to get a job . Upon hearing that he was working (even though he had achieved enough O levels to go to 6th Form the principal (C.L.C Mclennon) affectionately known by all Meadowbrook students as "SPANNA" who summoned him to her office at the school and told him that a young man of his potential don't need a job , he needs a career .

She proceeded to give him a letter which he took directly to Mico Teacher College where he was immediately enrolled and given a full Scholarship and a monthly stipend of $333.33 while attending for the next 3 years .

The Dread was happy that Freddy was going to Mico because he had planned that Freddy would take over the sports program at Meadowbrook eventually. He took the skills he had learnt from the Dread while still a player at Meadowbrook took Mico where Mico went on to win the inter collegiate Cricket Competition

Freddy did his internship at Waterford Primary where he established a sports program at the newly founded school and was influential in harnessing the cricket skills of West Indian cricketers Jermaine Lawson and Tamar Lambert.

After graduating at Mico he returned to his beloved Alma - mater Meadowbrook 1983 where he spent the next 2 years under the Dreads guidance and Spannas motherly protection where he learn and develop coaching skills which he ultimately took with him to JC and reestablished them into the power house in the sporting arena which they initially had in their earlier school history . While on the Meadowbrook faculty he was given a full schedule to teach History and Geography along with his PE duties which clearly diminished the impact he could have had at Meadowbrook even for that short 2 years .

While at Meadowbrook the other teacher started complaining that he was Ms. Mclennon ``pet" because he was allowed the latitude to be absent from staff meetings because he had commitment as a PE teacher which Spanna proudly announced to the other staff members before any inquiries were made of his

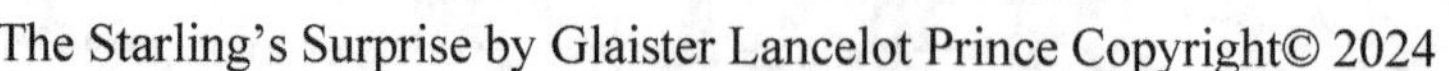

whereabouts. Ms. Mclennon clearly had ambitions of Freddy taking over the sports program at Meadowbrook someday to establish Meadowbrook as a sporting dynasty which would have made Meadowbrookonians proud .

In the short 2 years he spent at Meadowbrook he learned important lessons and strategies from the Dread which made him such an inspirational coach with JC and not Meadowbrook the beneficiary of his skill which would have disappointed Spanna and the Dread.

While being an understudy of the Dread he learned how to organize and set up the infrastructure of a PE department. He also realized the importance of that each player had a different mindset from him and he must recognize the difference if he was going to be successful in molding a sporting team to a successful championship . He also harnesses the skill of spotting and recruiting new players inside the school or outside of the institution .

One of the most important lessons he probably learned from the Dread was what Freddy called a points system which he established in the training sessions which identified the weakness and strength of players and where improvement was necessary . This was passed on to Freddy almost 40 years ago, and sophisticated computer programs are written today which gives sports teams the edge in their pursuit of championship . When Jimmy Adams (former West indies Cricket captain) saw Hitchcock implementing the Dread points system he was amazed at what Freddy was doing in his training regimen .

The Dread was 2 generations ahead of his time in his coaching methodology he used at Meadowbrook at what he passed on to his favorite student Alfred "Hitchcock " Henry . (This part of this book is written on October 23 2021 when former Manchester United player Gary Neville was bemoaning the fact that his beloved club was trashed by Liverpool 5-0 today at Old Trafford that they suffered their biggest defeat from their arch rival in 100 years because "they have been outrun by most team in the league ". He came to this conclusion after viewing Computer algorithms of Manchester United last 9 matches).

The Dread would have used his points system 40 years ago and use more impolite language than Gary Neville and simply said we were too lazy why we lost the match .

MR. HARE'S GOLDEN TOUCH - HIS UNWRITTEN SYSTEM

Mr. Hare was successful in all 3 schools he coached before coming to Meadowbrook in 1978 . He was successful in coaching Ruseas to winning the Headley Cup (Rural Area Schoolboy Cricket Champions) with Everton Coach and Errol Wilson being members of that team . He was responsible for setting up the development program at St Jago High School which won the Sunlight cup under the leadership of Gregory Brown .

Freddy also told me that he coached Meadowbrook Basketball Team which won the Division 2 basketball title with (Alton Crawford , Dave Hall, Conrad Davis, Harold Cameron , Carl Harris , Richard Chung, Ian Chung and Desmond Day are some of the players name I remember).

When Hitchcock left Meadowbrook and started coaching at JC in 1985 , he returned to his mentor (Mr Hare) to advise him on how to set up a scoring system for JC sports day because none existed at the time . (He coached Jimmy Adams while at JC who went on to captain the WEST INDIES CRICKET TEAM)He also talked him through a template (because no written one existed) on how to do a schedule for inter -house and inter-form competitions and with JC being a larger school than Meadowbrook it required a different scheduling and infrastructural system than what existed at Meadowbrook .

However the hidden reason why Mr. Hare was such a successful coach was organizing competitive matches inside and outside of the school for all the age groups .

When I was playing cricket, it seemed like we were playing competitive matches all the time . We were playing form matches , house matches , six a side competitions, Sunlight Cup matches , Minor cup, Evelyn Cup. He made sure that everybody got competitive matches under their belt, no matter the age group.

Looking back I now realize that he organize and ensured that we were playing competitively all the time blending the senior players with the younger players that everybody who came through that program were playing so much cricket , we became hardened school boy "professionals " that it no surprise that we dominated School boy cricket in the years he spent at Meadowbrook.

I am not sure this was consciously done but he ran the cricket program like a business enterprise. There are only 3 ways any business enterprise remain successful

1) Get new Customers
2) Get existing customers to buy more frequently
3) Get existing customers to buy more expensive products

Mr. Hare program always recruited

1) New players
2) Get existing players to improve their performance (Goosey (Stanford Brown and Hitchcock) came to Meadowbrook to play Football and they ended being an integral part of our dominance in cricket in the 1980s
3) Getting existing players to perform beyond their expectations

By time we won the Sunlight Cup in 1986 under the leadership of Kevin Reece , players such as Maurice Minott , Carlton Facey , Kirkton Ebanks and Hopeton Burke played with such professional dominance after being hardened by years of competitive matches that winning was a "Fait Accompli".

Freddy unconsciously took that system where he made JC the power house it became in school boy football after more than 2 decades in the doldrum . He was reflecting with me in our conversation that he had 25 players on his roster although ISSA rules allowed 22 players because he remembered Mr. Hare wisdom in keeping all the players in different age groups in active competition at all times . Whenever the opportunity presented itself to introduce a player who was too old for colts but not quite to the manning Cup level , he would introduce them into the match to sharpen their competitive edge and get valuable playing experience .

Mr. Hare did this all the time when we were playing Minor cup and Evelyn Cup matches every weekend which sharpened our professional edge and introduce youngsters who became dominant players on that 1986 Sunlight Cup team ,

Mr. Hare was also instrumental in organizing a " fourth form all-star competition amongst other high school coaches which kept the players too old for colts but not good enough for manning cup in a competitive professional environment which was adopted and implemented by ISSA as an official school boy competition

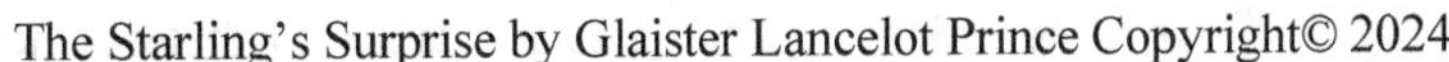

This may be one of the reasons why Jamaica is so dominant in Track and Field because there is no gap for a down time in the athletes because there is always an organized and structured competition for all age groups from primary school all the way to Class 1 at Champs every year .

Just imagine if a school implements a system which the Dread passed on to Alfred where all the Footballers or cricketers are organized to play competitive matches amongst their peers from first form to sixth form on a regular basis ?.

PASSING THE TORCH

Hitchcock spent 2 years at Meadowbrook under the tutelage of Mr. Hare from 1983-1985 where he assimilated a lot of the DREAD winning touch. During those years he helped groom some of the players who went on to dominate schoolboy cricket with Meadowbrook winning again in 1984 and 1986 and reaching the Sunlight Cup semi -finals every year until 1989. Hitchcock took Mr. Hare no nonsense approach to mental discipline which he recalled while at coach at JC he took out a player in a Manning Cup Match even though he had used up all the substitutes allowed. When the referee told him that he could not bring on a replacement player, he told the referee that he was going to play with 10 players because the player was mentally injured .

Hitchcock, like the Dread, had adopted the approach that it was better to leave out the disruptive and indiscipline player out of the team which affected the chemistry of the other players and play with a man short. This approach would have reverberated throughout the rest of the players knowing that no matter how talented they were they were not indispensable.

Unfortunately Hitchcock's stint at Meadowbrook was a short 2 years because he was getting better offers to coach at JC and more importantly the Principal (Ms. Mclennon "Spanna") who had treated him like her adopted son since he was a student in 1978 was suddenly and unceremoniously removed from the school. Ms. Mclennon's sudden and surprising departure was also followed by Mr. Hare leaving in 1986 . I am not privy to the reason behind Ms. Mclennon departure but her departure was a net negative for the culture at Meadowbrook and her love for

the school is summed up in a statement she made to Hitchcock in his short stint as a coach.

When the other teachers were mumbling about Hitchcock missing staff meetings because of coaching duties she confided in him that he was not to worry about the chattering because " some of these teachers were there for a job but YOU are MEADOWBROOK ". This statement confirmed that Ms. Mclennon probably had great plans to groom Hitchcock as sports master and ultimately into greater and more long term leadership at Meadowbrook.

However Meadowbrook lost was JC gain because his transition to JC was seamless with the help of his longtime friend and former JC student Ian "farrow" Forbes. Hitchcock knew "Farrow " since he was going to Grantham and Farrow was a student at JC captaining their Sunlight Cup Team. The JC community embraced him as one of their own but his first love was and still is MEADOWBROOK and he still reminisces the unconditional love he got from some teachers at Meadowbrook.

He remembered once when he had an ungainly and embarrassing Manning cup match at the National Stadium where because of the poor surface at the stadium he tripped on running to retrieve a ball in the 18 yard box which allowed Charlie Smith to win. We in the stands would not have been aware of the poor playing surface and he was mercilessly criticized to the point where he considered quitting. On the next match day he had no intention of playing and did not carry his playing gear.

Ms. Millwood (a teacher who also epitomizes the family spirit at Meadowbrook at the time) quietly spoke to Hitchcock and encouraged him not to quit and drove him to his home on Hughenden Ave so he could get his playing gear to play the match . **** Ms. Millwood was my form teacher when I first started Meadowbrook in 1974 and had 3 daughters who attended Meadowbrook during my time (Karen , Eleanor and Denise).

Hitchcock's first stint at JC was cut short when Family commitment and opportunity made him choose to migrate to the USA. However during his first stint at JC he was instrumental in introducing Michael Clark (successful track and field coach) to Farrow in 1989 upon meeting him at a Minor league match at D&G. That introduction ultimately reinvigorated the JC track and field program where it continues to be a force to be reckoned with at the ISSA Champs every year .

HITCHCOCK SUCCESS - THE DREAD GREATEST LEGACY

During his years away in the states he kept in touch with his friends Ian Forbes and John Mair (former Olympian track and field 100 meter, who also went to Meadowbrook and JC). In their yearly trip to the Penn relays they would link up and stay in touch and constantly remind him a place was always there waiting for him at JC. When his daughter graduated from Spelman College in 2005 he decided to restart his coaching duties back at JC.

However during his absence JC had reestablished their dominance in track and field . (They won 6 ISSA BOYS "CHAMPS" in the 1990s after winning for the first time in 32 years in 1991.) Hitchcock had set up the infrastructure for a professionally run sports day in his original tenure in charge with the help and guidance of Mr. HARE. This infrastructure would have been in place when Michael Clarke took over as JC track and field coach in 1989 following his introduction to the JC community by Hitchcock . The rest as we would say is history as JC took those foundations built by Hitchcock in the 1980s and dominated " Boys Champs " in the 1990s.

Hitchcock's successful return to JC is well documented (winning the manning cup after a 33 year absence , winning the walker cup for the first time in the school history and triple champions for the first time in the school history.

The trophies he won at JC was as a result of the continued groundwork he built upon his return in 2005 which captured the attention of the school board chaired by Danny Williams who was impressed by the systems Hitchcock was putting in place at JC and started giving financial support to his program which led to the explosive growth of their sporting program with the Ashenheim Stadium being the pinnacle of that success thus far.

When Hitchcock started his JC career in 1985 , there was no sports day at JC and with the help and the guidance from Mr. Hare he laid the foundation for establishing a sports program which led to the revival of JC as a sporting powerhouse amongst Jamaican High Schools.

When he returned in 2005 after a long absence , he picked up where he had left off and continued to introduce the systems he had learned from the DREAD as a student and an PE coach at Meadowbrook in the 1980s. He took the DREAD

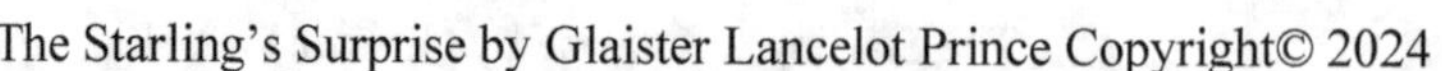

winning formula that he learnt at Meadowbrook and created enormous success at JC who had a much larger student body and a more potent alumni . Hitchcock quotes " every challenge that came up while he was at JC he would draw back on what he had learnt from the DREAD".

Hitchcock said he focused on football in his second stay at JC because during his time living in the USA he was assisting the JC football program during the off season after being encouraged by his longtime friends Ian Forbes and John Mair .

Some of the systems he implemented were
1) An end of year review and community service awards for his players
2) End of year presentation based on his points system
3) Implementing a points system during his training regimen .
4) Weekly discussion with his coaching staff on what should be done on a monthly, weekly and daily basis for each form .
5) Giving senior players the responsibility for younger players by allowing them to document their performance at training
6) Letting his players and coaching staff that they had to focus on the 3 As if they wanted to be a part of his program . The (3As) were Attitude , Ambition and Ability in that order.

These were just some of the systems Hitchcock implemented during his successful tenure at JC which he learnt from the DREAD . I encouraged him to start writing down all his systems to put in a formal template which he can brand and use for himself to set up successful coaching programs for himself anywhere in the world.

HITCHCOCK AND ISSA

Hitchcock's relationship with ISSA is well documented in the media which is skewed towards giving ISSA side of the story . Knowing that there are normally 3 sides to every story (your side , my side and the truth) I ask Hitchcock to present his side of his relationship with ISSA .

After listening to Hitchcock these are my conclusions:

1) Alfred was standing up for the wellbeing and the future of the school athletes .

2) ISSA and their private sector sponsors are more concerned about the money being made than the wellbeing of the athletes .

In closing it is my opinion that Hitchcock is ahead of his time in advocating for the wellbeing of his players and a time will come , hopefully in the near future where athletes and parents are compensated for the enormous amount of money being generated by their ability at a particular sport , instead of not being given a seat at the table when the resources accumulated are been distributed.

MEADOWBROOK UNIQUE GIFT

Meadowbrook is a small co-educational school which meant that we had a population of both sexes (boys and girls) of about less than 700 during the 1970s and 1980s with more female than male .(* Meadowbrook school population January 2022 is about 1400)

One of the Dread special gifts that made Meadowbrook such a competitive school during those years was the ability to turn footballers into cricketers . The athlete who best epitomized this more than any other was Anthony Reynolds or Tony Reynolds. Nobody called him Tony or Reynolds like most others even today when anyone talks about him it's Tony Reynolds.

Tony Reynolds came to Meadowbrook to play in the Manning Cup and he was a graceful winger who glided over tackles like an Olympic hurdler and sprinted across the football field like a greyhound .

He was a multi-talented athlete who was encouraged by his football teammate Alfred "Hitchcock" Henry to try out for the Sunlight cup cricket team . He was so successful that when we reached our first semifinal in our school history he was the wicketkeeper and a graceful middle order batsman who timed the ball with ease.

His wicketkeeping exploits were a joy to watch as sometimes in training and some matches (if Mr. Hare ever allowed him) he would stand directly behind the stumps to the lightning pace of Glen Atkins and sometimes stumped batsmen who were stranded out of their crease against our fast bowlers. Only the former Boys

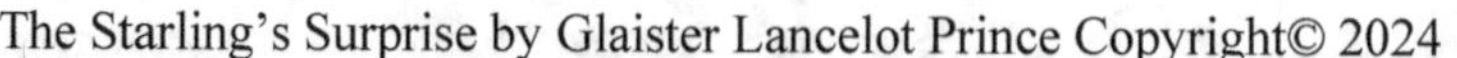

Town Multi-talented footballer and cricketer Herbert "Dago" Gordon , I ever witnessed "standing up " to fast bowlers at a senior level.

Another of the various athletes who represented Meadowbrook at both Football and Cricket was Maurice Minott 'Mighty Mouse".

It is no surprise that with a nickname like Mighty Mouse he would perform well at cricket. That nickname was the nickname of the former Boys Town , Jamaica and West Indies cricket great whose career was cut short by an unfortunate car accident in 1959 in England. It is reported that Smith who was only 26 at the time of his death and that some 60,000 people attended his funeral in Jamaica.

Minott was an aggressive opening batsman on the 1984 and 1986 winning Sunlight Cup team who controlled aggression and confidence was a pleasure to watch. He was also the right wing back on our winning Walker Cup and Nutrament Shield team in 1985.

FORGOTTEN SUPPORT

This part of our journey to our storybook success was almost forgotten if it were not for 2 of my lifelong friends who were also part of this rags to riches story (Lenworth "Jago" Johnson and Christopher "Chris" Cheddar). After asking Jago to read a draft of my book he reminded me of the integral part that the school feeding program played to most of our athletes and the role that Mrs. Chung played (Richard and Ian Chung's mother) in opening up her house and her kitchen to some of the best home cooked food in Havendale along Chevy Chase.

Mrs. Chung home was ideally situated along the short cut from the school to (bottom field) and most of our cricketers would stop after training by that house along Chevy Chase and a warm meal was always ready which was always welcomed by all teenagers who had just completed a tough training session at bottom field .

Mrs. Chung's model of providing a well cooked meal for our players was formalized by THE DREAD , with the help of Gerry Belnavis who was instrumental in arranging to get the required food to cook from the owner of HAROLD SUPERMARKET who attended most of our matches. (* A number of

top tier schools have now adopted a school feeding program as an integral part of their athletic program)

Thanks to Christopher Cheddar who reminded me of the teachers who were instrumental in getting the food cooked (The late Mrs. Melody Russell, Mrs. Blossom Laidlaw, Mrs. Helen Bromley).

I would be remiss if I wrote about forgotten support without a special mention to our groundsman at bottom field. The late Mr. Barnes (REDS) was the groundsman who was responsible for the upkeep of (bottom field) and responsible for preparing the cricket pitch for our competitive matches and all the athletes who knew and remembered REDS have lots of great memories of his contribution.

EPILOGUE

If the material written in this book inspires one alumni to write or speak their own story or inspires just one current or future student to find the courage to compete or support a friend to compete , it may make a new group of students , in the words of Steel Pulse "RALLY ROUND THE GREEN AND BLUE "

COPYRIGHTED ©

SOME HISTORIC SPORTS TEAMS OF MEADOWBROOK HIGH SCHOOLS
(NEXT PAGES)

First Football Team – Principal, Mr. Whitmarh Knight

Rear L-R: Errol Henry, Jean Royale, Norman Dubisette, Kenneth Clarke, Neil Myrie, Henrick Hamilton, George Thompson, ?,?. Front L-R: Robin McGhie, Hugh Jureidini, Mr Whitmarsh-Knight - second Principal, Mr. Millet -sportsmaster, Lyndon Facey, Peter Boxer. Seated in front with ball: Dennis

First Cricket Team

Rear L-R: Henrick Hamilton, ?, Jean Royale, Neil Myrie, Sammy ?, Errol Latty, Peter Boxer. Front L-R: Errol Henry, Norman Dubisette, Mr Whitmarsh-Knight - second Principal, Mr. Millet - sportsmaster, Hugh Jureidini, Ruel Playfair Scott.

1984 Sunlight Cup Champions

Standing L to R…
Kevin Reese, Mark Wiggan, Paul Brown, John Harvey Devon McDonald, Paul Smith, Donald Thomas, Maurice Minott and Leon Johnson

In front, (left to right)
Clive Edwards, Garfield Marston, Carlton Facey, Dirk Dewar and Kirkton Ebanks

1986 Sunlight and Tappin Cup Champions

Standing in back (left to right)

Mr. D Gordon, Mark Wiggan, Donald Farquharson, Paul Brown, Paul Smith, Radgh Mason, Devon Miller Maurice White and Mr. Rory McGregor

Seated front (left to right)

Maurice Minott, Kirkton Ebanks, Kevin Reese, Carlton Facey, Dillion Ebanks, Hopeton Burke

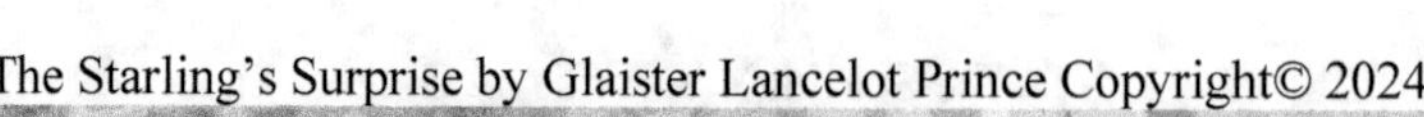

Calabar seek to avenge '82 defeat by Meadowbrook

Sunlight Cup cricket final today

The Inter-Secondary schools Sunlight Cup cricket final between Meadowbrook and Calabar begins this morning at Sabina Park starting at 11 o'clock. Play will continue tomorrow and Wednesday if necessary.

This year's final will be a repeat of 1982's when Meadowbrook defeated Calabar to gain their first hold on the Cup.

Meadowbrook, who topped Zone 'A' of the competition, advanced to the final by virtue of a 12-run victory over Kingston College last Tuesday in one of the two semi-final playoffs. On the same day Calabar, who are also from Zone 'A' defeated Tarrant Cup limited-over champions St. Andrew Technical by 48 runs in the other semi-final encounter to earn their berth.

On the strength of their performances this season, Calabar seemingly possess the better all round team. Their depth was evident last week when they turned the tables on highly fancied STATHS, who had earlier defeated them in the Tarrant Cup semis.

Meadowbrook, not to be outdone, showed admirable fighting qualities to dispose of KC after being restricted to 125. They are yet to lose a game this season, but cannot be said to be as impressive as Calabar in victory. When both teams met earlier this season the game ended in a draw.

When all is said, cricket finals at this level are often won by teams that hold on to their catches and it is in this area that the fortunes of either side will depend.

Calabar will be captained by all-rounder Mark Baker, the sole survivor of the 1982 losing team. And Meadowbrook will be skippered by Garfield Marston, who leads the batting averages in this year's competition.

Baker, an opening batsman and useful wrist spinner, has been the most consistent run-getter for Calabar this season. Last Tuesday he took five for 45 against STATHS to emerge his team's leading bowler.

Apart from Baker, Calabar will be looking to opener Orville Brown, Brian Blair, Nehemiah Perry, Audley Boyd and colts player Darren Laidlaw to get among the runs. Young Laidlaw topscored with 55 last week.

The bowling will be centered around pacemen Paul Raphael, Roger Robotham and Ralston Bailey with support coming from spinners Baker, Perry and Donovan Simon.

Meadowbrook, on the other hand, will counter with batsmen Marston, opener Leon Johnson and Chris Cheddar as well as Dirk Dewar, Kirton Ebanks, Paul Smith and Kevin Reese, who led the way against KC. Their bowling will more than likely be spearheaded by offspinner Devon McDonald, who came into prominence against KC by taking 7 for 18 in 23 overs, 12 of which were maidens.

McDonald got the ball to turn considerably and is again expected to pose problems for the batsmen. Medium pacers Edwards and Dewar should provide useful support, along with Marston and Cheddar.

Meadowbrook Sunlight Cup champions

Displaying great determination, Meadowbrook won the Sunlight Cup cricket competition for the second time in three years when they scored a thrilling four-run victory over Calabar in the two-day final (replay) which ended at Sabina Park yesterday.

Calabar, beaten by Meadowbrook in the 1982 final, failed in their bid to avenge that defeat after restricting their opponents to a low score on Friday.

The previous final earlier in the week was rained out on the second day after Meadowbrook were bowled out for 167.

Final scores were: Meadowbrook 100, Calabar 96.

Resuming at their overnight score of 78 for six, Calabar who last won the Cup in 1946 when they were joint holders with St. George's College, lost their seventh wicket in the morning's first over when overnight batsman Audley Boyd went without scoring. He played back to a ball from offspinner Dirk Dewar and was adjudged leg before to make it 78 for seven.

Mark Henry, who was 14 not out overnight, was then joined by Ralston Bailey and the pair slowly pushed the score along to take their team within sight of victory. However, with the score on 95, Bailey was deceived by a ball from offspinner Devon McDonald and was beautifully stumped by Carlton Facey for 15.

With the game now delicately poised, McDonald struck again in the same over by bowling Paul Raphael for zero to make it 95 for nine. Calabar were hoping at this stage that the last pair of Henry and Roger Robotham would have pulled it off, but with five runs needed for victory Robotham offered a solid return catch to 15-year-old left-arm spinner Kirton Ebanks, thus signalling the end after 45 minutes play. Henry, who defended stubbornly, was 1 not out.

Bowling for Meadowbrook, Ebanks, who had taken three for 18 on Friday, finished with four for 31 off 15.3 overs, four of which were maidens. McDonald took two for 18 in eleven overs, Dewar one for 22 and medium pacer Clive Edwards one for eleven.

Meadowbrook's captain Garfield Marston was presented with the Sunlight Cup after the match by H Taylor, chairman of the Sunlight Cup competition and Headmaster of Jamaica College, the school which won the Cup last year.

Marston and his team-mates duly ran a victory lap around the world famous cricket ground.

Meadowbrook, who are undefeated this season, may now meet the winner of the Headley Cup competition for Rural schools in the Sunlight Cup playoff to decide the Inter-Secondary All Island cricket champions for 1984.

Meadowbrook snatch Sunlight Cup

Meadowbrook emerged the 1984 Inter-Secondary Schools Sunlight Cup cricket champions last Saturday when they defeated Calabar by four runs in a low scoring final over two days at Sabina Park.

Scores were: Meadowbrook 100, Calabar 96.

It was the second time in three years that Meadowbrook were winning the Sunlight Cup, having defeated Calabar in the 1982 final to gain their very first hold on the Cup.

Electing to bat after winning the toss on Friday, Meadowbrook found themselves in trouble at 30 for four, as paceman Roger Robotham ripped through the top of the batsmen.

Meadowbrook, however, managed to reach 100 through the efforts of Chris Cheddar (30), Carlton Facey (17), skipper Garfield Marston (10) and opener Leon Johnson (10).

Bowling for Calabar, Robotham finished with 4 for 25, offspinner Nehemiah Perry 4 for 20, Audley Boyd 1 for 10, and Paul Raphael 1 for 10.

Starting their reply at 3:45 on Friday afternoon, Calabar, chasing what appeared a modest score, failed to get on top of the situation after occupying the crease for 165 minutes on Friday afternoon.

They ended the day struggling at 78 for six, losing two of those wickets via the run out route, and Mark Baker, the Calabar skipper and opening batsman, for 37 in the closing minutes of play.

On Saturday morning, Meadowbrook ran an early break through when overnight batsman Audley Boyd was dismissed for zero by Dirk Dewar in the first over. That dismissal signalled the beginning of the end for Calabar as they limited by five runs. Mark Henry was left undefeated with 1.

Bowling for Meadowbrook, left-arm spinner Kirton Ebanks took 4 for 31, offspinner Devon McDonald 2 for 18, Dirk Dewar 1 for 22, and Clive Edwards 1 for 11.

The two-day encounter was really a replay, the scheduled final was affected by rain weather after Meadowbrook were dismissed for 167 with Kevin Reese getting 77 not out.

Sunlight Cup final interestingly poised

At the end of the first's day play in the Sunlight Cup cricket final replay at Sabina Park, Calabar in reply to Meadowbrook's score of 100 were struggling at 77 for six. The match continues this morning, legspinner Audley this week, survived two chances before he was bowled leg stump by Robotham for eight.

Bowling for Calabar, Robotham finished with four for 25 in 12 overs, offspinner Nehemiah Perry four for 20 in 9.2 overs, legspinner Audley Boyd one for ten and medium pacer Paul Raphael one for 19.

Calabar in their reply lost wickets at 8, 33, 43, 44, 59 and 77 as only skipper Mark Baker (37) showed any real resistance.

It was Meadowbrook who won the toss and elected to bat on an uneven strip. They soon ran into problems by losing their first four wickets with only 30 runs on the board, as paceman Roger Robotham made the early breakthrough.

Meadowbrook lost their fifth wicket with the score on 46, but number three batsman Christopher Cheddar (30) and Carlton Facey (17) batting at number seven, held Calabar at bay with a fighting sixth wicket partnership.

On Facey's departure, the remaining batsmen fell cheaply. Earlier, opener Leon Johnson and skipper Garfield Marston made ten each.

MEADOWBROOK WALKER CUP WIN 1986

1986 Walker Cup and Nutrament Shields Champions

Standing (L-R):

Coach: Putt Williams, Paul "Gobbler 2" Smith, Emille "Dango" Campbell, Andre "Goody" Goodison, Stephen "Cluck" Coombs, Uri White, Patrick "Gobbler 1" Smith, Lorne Kirlew, Devon "Tweedo" Reid, Raymond "Bobby/Truck" Smith, Teacher/Manager: Donat Gordon, Courtney Strudwick
Stooping:
Radgh Mason, Kingsley Bernard, Luke Witter, Maurice Minnott, David "Balla" Brown, Billy "Russian" Lyons.
Goalkeepers:
Alwayne "Tutu" Rose and Vill Jeffrey

1982 Colts Team
Runners up

Standing (L-R):
Kevin "Bungle" Barnes, Paul "Gobbler 2" Smith, Patrick "Gobbler 1" Smith,
Maurice "izmo" Minnott, Stephen "Stadium Gyal" Williams, Leon "Buffy"
Chambers, Robert Saltau, Leon "Johno" Johnson, Hopeton "Hitchie" Burke
Stooping:
Luke Witter, Orlando "Ricky" Thompson, Anthony Moore, Spencer Wong, Kirk
"Squitty" Smith, Steve Jones, Peter "Goldilocks" Sinclair
Goalkeepers:
Errol "Silly" Silvera and Kirk Doaman

1983 Manning Cup Team
Standing (L-R):
Hopeton English, Richard Lodge, Patrick "Gobbler 1" Smith, Benton Morris, Paul "Gobbler 2" Smith, Steve Bull, Andrew "Bird" Earle
Stooping (L-R): Michael "Lookup" Lindsay, Luke Witter, Anthony Moore, Leon "Johno" Johnson, Everton "Boom" Ricketts, Lester King
Goalkeepers:
Noel "Tippy" Clarke and Carlton Facey
Missing:
Alan Blackwood, Howie Smith and Kurt Campbell.

1984 Manning Cup Team

Standing (L-R):
Peter "Goldilocks" Sinclair, Richard Lodge, Devon "Tweedo" Reid, Steve Bull, Hopeton English, Benton Morris, Kirk "Squitty" Smith, Raymond "Bobby/Truck" Smith, Leon "Buffy" Chambers
Stooping (L-R):
Paul "Gobbler 2" Smith, Patrick "Gobbler 1" Smith, Howie Smith, Leon "Johno" Johnson, Dirk Dewar, Michael "Lookup" Lindsay, Luke Witter, Anthony Moor
Goalkeepers:
Errol "Silly" Silvera, Noel "Tippy" Clarke

1985 Manning Cup Team

Standing:

Raymond "Bobby/Truck" Smith, Luke Witter, Maurice Minnott, Billy "Russian" Lyons, Harvey Plumber, Patrick "Gobbler 1" Smith, Raymond Robinson
Stooping (L-R):
Orlando "Ricky" Thompson, Devon "Tweedo" Reid, Michael "Lookup" Lindsay, Uri White, Emille "Dango" Campbell, Leon "Johno" Johnson
Goalkeepers:
Noel "Tippy" Clarke and Alwayne "Tutu" Rose
Missing:
Paul "Gobbler 2" Smith

Figure 1 Picture of Glaister Prince and Former Meadowbrook High School Principal Mr. Bogle in January 2024